Building And Flying Model Aircraft

Robert Schleicher and James R. Barr

Dover Publications, Inc.

New York

Published in Canada by General Publishing Company,
Ltd., 30 Lesmill Road, Don Mills, Toronto, Ontario.

This Dover edition, first published in 1988, is an unabridged and slightly corrected republication of the work
originally published by Chilton Book Company, Radnor,
Pennsylvania, in 1980. The "Sources of Supply" section has
been updated for the present edition.

Manufactured in the United States of America
Dover Publications, Inc., 31 East 2nd Street, Mineola, N.Y.
11501

Library of Congress Cataloging-in-Publication Data

Schleicher, Robert H.
    Building and flying model aircraft / by Robert
Schleicher and James R. Barr.
        p.   cm.
    "An unabridged and slightly corrected republication of
the work originally published by Chilton Book Company,
Radnor, Pennsylvania, in 1980"—T.p. verso.
    Bibliography: p.
    Includes index.
    ISBN 0-486-25801-7 (pbk.)
    1. Airplanes—Models. I. Barr, James R. II. Title.
TL770.S328 1988
629.133′134—dc19   88-16177
                                                                CIP

Contents

Chapter 1   **The Wings of Man**   1
       Flight Forms   2
       Air Power Plants   4
       Costs   5
       Ready-Built Models   10
       True-to-Life Scale Models   11

Chapter 2   **Basic Aerodynamics**   14
       The Basic Principle   14
       The Secret of the Birds   15
       Climbing High   17
       In-Flight Stability   19
       Searching for CG   22
       Complete Control   23
       Lighter-than-Air Paints and "Skins"   27

Chapter 3   **Power Plants**   28
       The Internal Combustion Engine   28
       Starting Techniques   31
       Selecting the Proper Fuel   37
       Fuel Tanks   37
       Mufflers   38
       Choosing Engines and Propellers   38
       Electric Power Plants   39
       Tow-Line Engines   43

Chapter 4   **Fly-by-Wire**   47
       The Flight Line School   47
       Your First Solo   49
       The Model Aerodrome   50
       Control Lines   52
       Stepping Up   53
       Simple Stunts   56
       Combat   61

Contents

Chapter 5 **Radio Control**   62
      Radios   62
      Channels   63
      Frequencies   65
      Quality Bargains   69
      Radio Installation   70
      Servo Motor Mounts   71

Chapter 6 **Flight Magic**   76
      The No-Crash System   76
      Your First Radio-Control Aircraft   78
      The First Flight   80
      Happy Landings   83
      Advanced Flying Techniques   84
      Aileron Rolls   87
      Pattern Flying   88
      Thermal Soaring   88

Chapter 7 **Free Flight**   90
      Classes   90
      Peanut and Jumbo Scale   91
      Indoor Flight   93
      Trim Tabs   95
      Rubber Power   95
      Outdoor Free Flight   97

Chapter 8 **Helicopters**   102
      Hovering Flight   102
      Forward Flight   104
      Radio-Control Helicopters   105
      Autorotation   108
      Helicopter Flight   109

Chapter 9 **Kit Building**   111
      Cement Secrets   111
      Instant Glue Joints   112
      Epoxies   115
      Tools   118
      Control Surfaces   120

Chapter 10 **Paint and Other Finishes**   122
      Tissue Paper Covering   122
      Plastic Color Coverings   124
      Painting Techniques   128

	Decal Markings	129
	Repair Tips	131
	Showroom-Fresh Tips	133

Chapter 11   Super Scale   **134**

	Determining Scale	134
	Scale Performance	134
	The Scale Effect	137
	Cheap Scale	139
	Control-Line Scale	139
	Radio-Control Scale	139

Chapter 12   Clubs and Competition   **143**

	Local Clubs	143
	Academy of Model Aeronautics	144
	National Model Airplane Championships	145
	The Rules	148

Glossary   **153**

Sources of Supply, Publications and Clubs   **157**

	Sources of Supply	157
	Publications	160
	Clubs	161

Index   **163**

Building
And Flying
Model
Aircraft

Chapter 1

✈
The Wings of Man

The dream of freedom often includes the dream of flight. The whole concept of being "as free as a bird" is so strong in many of us that one wonders if, perhaps, man really was meant to fly. The fantasy of flight has haunted man since the beginning of recorded time; countless legends, gods imbued with the power to fly, and biblical references to man's flight predate the actual event. For those of us who would rather risk time and money, rather than life and limb, building and flying model aircraft may be the ideal fulfillment of a fantasy.

The hobby encompasses a number of delights and certainly is not limited to "toy" airplanes. This is one leisure activity that involves enough time outdoors to qualify as a sport for the whole family. You'll get about as much exercise flying a radio-control (R/C) or a control-line (C/L) model aircraft as you would sailing a small boat. Flying model aircraft can be a more fascinating hobby if you build your own models, but there are dozens of truly excellent quick-to-build and almost-ready-to-fly models, and almost every hobby shop offers built-up kit models and often provide a building service. If you prefer the hobby aspect, there's plenty of challenge available, ranging from the assembly of simple kits that can be completed on a single Saturday to built-from-plans exact-scale models that might take a year or more to finish.

Many pilots of full-size private and commercial aircraft feel that flying a model aircraft actually provides more freedom and enjoyment than flying the real thing. There are, for example, no complex regulations to worry about with model aircraft and only a fraction of the investment to risk when you attempt an aerobatic maneuver. Hundreds of hours of very expensive practice are needed to solo in a real aircraft and you have to pass some pretty grueling written and flight tests. You can duplicate those flying maneuvers with a model aircraft, however, after only a few months of practice. Potential insurance problems are taken care of when you join the Academy of Model Aeronautics (AMA). The AMA membership provides liability insurance as part of the package, and it applies anywhere you fly as long as you are flying according to the AMA safety

Fig. 1-1 A Flyline Models' radio-control Fairchild 22 preparing to land.
Courtesy Flyline Models.

code, a copy of which you'll receive with your membership (it is sometimes changed, to comply with the insurance company regulations, so don't rely on just the "safety code" shown here). In all, there's more freedom, relaxation and exciting fun in flying model aircraft than you'll find anywhere.

Flight Forms

You can envision your model aircraft any way that pleases you. Consider it your own little bird who flies exactly where and how you wish you could, or consider your model to be full-size and shrink yourself enough to imagine yourself in the cockpit. Most model aircraft enthusiasts imagine both situations at one time or another. The choice of model aircraft will place more or less emphasis on the "bird" or "cockpit" flights of fancy. The airplanes that are launched with no form of remote control are called "free-flight" models, and they are certainly the closest thing you'll get to a bird. The other extreme of the hobby is occupied with flying model aircraft where the rudder (for right and left turns), the elevator (for up and down movements), the ailerons (the movable flying surfaces that roll the plane into a right or left bank), the engine speed, and sometimes even retractable landing gear, dive brakes, or bomb bay doors are all controlled by a radio transmitter sending signals to a radio receiver on board the aircraft. There are, to be sure, less complicated radio-control model aircraft, just as there are more complex free-flight models, but this will give you a hint of the possible range this hobby encompasses.

More control-line model airplanes are sold than any other. Firms like Cox and Testors sell millions of their inexpensive fuel-powered plastic model airplanes in toy and hobby stores and departments every year. Most control-line models have a simple lever inside the plane (called a "bell crank") that is pushed or pulled by a lever in the full-size flier's hand. The two levers are connected by two nylon cords or steel cables that are each 10 to 70 feet long. When the flier cocks the lever (called a "control handle") forward or backward, the tow lines force the bell crank in the model airplane to move a corresponding distance. The bell crank is, in turn, connected by a steel rod (called a "push rod") to a pivot point on the elevator to give the flier full control over the plane's up-and-down

Fig. 1-2 Simple almost-ready-to-fly control-line models, like this Cox Stuka, offer incredible realism. *Courtesy Cox Hobbies.*

movement during flight. The engine speed remains on full until the power plant runs out of fuel. The rudder is canted to the right to keep the two flying lines taut for full flier control. The airplane will then fly around and around the circle until it runs out of gas or until the flier forces it to land (or crashes it). The flier has only elevator control with a control-line model aircraft, but that is enough to allow virtually any type of aerobatic maneuver from a simple loop to advanced stunt flights. Experienced control-line modelers can even place two or more fliers in the center of the circle so each person controls one plane. The two fliers then stage mock combat or duplicate the maneuvers of aerobatic formation flying.

Air Power Plants

You can duplicate just about any type of full-size aircraft you wish with a flying model. Almost any of them are available as inexpensive ready-to-fly models, simple kits, or complex kits including both powered and non-powered types. The limitations of the control lines restrict this type of model aircraft to the powered types, but you can find just about anything from a scale-model piper cub to a multi-engined bomber to special "stunt" planes that will actually outperform the prototype aircraft. Most modelers, even the most experienced, use the simple single-cylinder two-stroke engines, but there are some ducted-fan two-strokes that perform like jet engines and a few planes that utilize actual jet engines. Stick to the simple engines with propellers for now; if you need blinding speed, then try model rockets with "vehicles" designed for ultimate speed, performance—you'll have trouble enough learning to fly an aircraft at the speeds that the tiny .020 or .049-cubic-inch displacement engines allow. Engines up to about 2.6-cubic-inch displacement are available for those who demand really gigantic planes, and some of the .61-cubic-inch engines have enough power to pull a lightweight model to a genuine 150 miles an hour.

The free-flight and radio-control model aircraft ready-to-fly and kit selection includes every imaginable type of full-size aircraft from biplanes of the World War I era to helicopters to four-engined bombers to powered gliders or sailplanes. The same two-stroke internal combustion power plants that power the control-line models are used for the radio-control models and many of the free-flight aircraft miniatures. Electric motors, powered by rechargeable on-board ni-cad (nickel-cadmium) batteries are becoming increasingly popular with radio-control modelers, thanks to the quiet simplicity of the motors. The non-powered gliders are launched by on-the-ground "engines" like the elastic band (actually surgical tubing) "Hi-Start" sold by Cox and others or by electric winches. These "engines" simply pull the aircraft forward, and lift created by the model's wings carries it upward about 400 feet into the air. An experienced free-flight modeler can build and launch an airplane that will stay in the air for 10

Fig. 1-3   An electric winch (in the box) is used to launch some radio-control sailplanes.
This is the Cox "Olympic II".

minutes or more; a radio-controlled sailplane can be kept in the air for an
hour. Most sailplane modelers are happy enough with five-minute flights,
however.

Costs

The amount of money you spend on a flying model aircraft will
depend mostly on how much control you expect to have over it and just
how closely you want to match (or improve on) the performance of the

full-size aircraft. The least expensive models are the balsa wood hand-launched gliders that sell for about a dollar. The cost can range upward to $1000 or more for an exact-scale twin-engined bomber with a seven-channel radio-control rig. The cost will depend somewhat on whether you are willing to build the model from a kit or if you want it to be ready to fly. If we were to rank model airplanes by cost category, then the free-flight aircraft would certainly be the least expensive, followed by the control-line powered models, then radio-control gliders or sailplanes, and finally the most expensive radio-control powered aircraft. There's a considerable amount of price overlap among the categories; the best free-flight models with timers can cost as much as $200, while you can buy a ready-to-fly Cox R/C "E-Z Bee" powered radio-control trainer or an inexpensive kit and a two-channel radio for only $150 to $200.

Free-Flight Models

That dollar hand-launched glider is the simplest form of a free-flight model. There are kits that will allow you to carry the concept of non-controlled flight all the way to a 12-foot wingspan. The larger gliders can be launched by hand just like that simple balsa wood sheet model, but there are better ways of doing the job, including a 150-foot-long line on a reel to pull the model over your head while you run into the wind in much the same way you would launch a kite. There are also some free-flight

Fig. 1-4   Peck-Polymers "Prairie Bird" is one of the better beginner model kits for indoor and outdoor free flight. *Courtesy Peck-Polymers.*

models that have fuel-powered .049-cubic-inch displacement (also called "Half A" or "½A") engines to carry them into the air. Free flight includes those balsa wood stick models with tissue paper coverings and rubber band-powered propellers. The smaller balsa wood stick models can even be flown indoors. Most free-flight kits range in price from about $2 to $12, but some of the larger models of real aircraft and the"competition" free-flight kits can run as much as $80. Most of the kits that have rubber bands to power the propeller can be modified to accept the fuel-burning engines. The engine will run between $10 and $100, depending on the size and whether or not you have to have one of the hand-fitted and tuned "competition" engines. A timer, for the release of the stabilizer to "dethermalize" the model so it won't fly completely out of sight, can run another $2 to $50, again depending on whether you want a simple cloth rope "fuse" or a complex wind-up "competition" timer.

Control-Line Models

For a beginning control-line model $25 to $35 is a good range to consider. You can buy one of the Cox or Testors ready-to-fly plastic planes for as little as $15. The lantern battery to provide ignition power for starting and fuel will run another $5 or so. The larger Cox ready-to-fly planes run in the $25-to-$30 range and, for that price, you can buy one of the simple sheet balsa wood kits (that can be assembled in about three hours or less), an .049-cubic-inch displacement engine, control lines, control handle, cement, colored paint, and clear paint. Be certain that your first control model is either marked for "beginners" or that it is called a "trainer" so you'll stand a chance, at least, of learning to fly it before you crash it. Intermediate and "stunt" control-line models with larger engines will run in the $50-to-$100 range and that's about where most modelers stop. If you're really bitten by the control-line bug, you may want to advance to control-line scale, speed, or combat models and invest more in a single aircraft and engine.

Radio-Control Sailplanes

Most books and magazines lump all types of radio-control models into one category. We feel, however, that there is such a vast difference between powered radio-control model aircraft and radio-control sailplanes that the sailplanes are virtually in a category of their own. We do feel that the electric motor-powered sailplanes, like those made by Cox, Graupner, and Astro Flight, belong in the non-powered category. The electric motors, like the engines in the free-flight aircraft models, are there strictly to get the plane well clear of the ground where winds and rising air currents or thermals can sustain its flight. The major item of expense with any radio-controlled model is going to be the radio transmitter and receiver. You can keep that cost to a minimum with a sailplane, because you really need only two channels—one to operate the elevator (for up and down control) and another to operate the rudder (for right and left). Some of the more advanced sailplane modelers add a third channel for the control of ailerons (for banking) and even a fourth for the control of the tow line release or, perhaps, retractable landing gear. Frankly, we feel that the third and fourth channels are a luxury that's not really worth considering for the newcomer. That simple two-channel radio and receiver setup will cost between $80 and $150 (depending mostly on the quality and power or range), and you can use it in every sailplane you make, since the radio will usually survive crashes that can destroy the aircraft. The glider or sailplane itself will run between $20 and $100 as a kit.

Powered Radio-Control Aircraft

Radio control allows the modeler to build an aircraft that looks exactly like the real thing with no control-line wires to spoil its effect. The recent advances in electronic circuitry also permit the modeler to control his aircraft with virtually the same amount of precision as if he or she were in the cockpit. The cost of a powered radio-control aircraft can be less than $150 if you're willing to settle for the single-channel (rudder) control of a beginner's ready-to-fly like the Cox "E-Z Bee." If you build your own from a kit designed for one of the .020 or .049-cubic-inch engines and a two-channel lightweight radio receiver and transmitter, you may get by for less than $200. These smaller aircraft will probably have a wingspan in the 30-to-50-inch range. The typical radio-controlled aircraft have wingspans in the 50-to-60-inch range with designs that call for an engine

Fig. 1-5   Monte Peecher guides his radio-control Sig "Kiwi" just before takeoff.

Fig. 1-6   A high-wing aircraft makes a fine "trainer" for powered radio-control flying.

with .20 to .61 cubic inch of displacement. Most modelers want aileron control for banked turns and throttle control as well as elevator and rudder control, so a radio transmitter and receiver with four or more channels is necessary. These aircraft are built from kits, and the model and engine will run $70 or more while the radio will cost $200 or more. Most modelers end up spending closer to $500 for their second or third powered radio-control model. Remember, though, that the radio transmitter and receiver can be used in your next aircraft simply by disconnecting and removing the receiver, the servos (that actually operate the control surfaces), and throttle from the aircraft.

If you spend more than $500, you can get into some of the truly exotic radio-control aircraft like twin-engined models, ducted fan-engined "jets", or radio-control helicopters. With few exceptions, however, these more costly aircraft are far more difficult to fly than the "beginner" models in that $100-to-$500 price range. This is one hobby where investing more dollars can actually make the flying more difficult—but that greater degree of difficulty is just the kind of challenge a hobbyist often desires. Just be warned that you're much wiser to learn to fly with one of the inexpensive powered radio-control models before writing a check or signing a charge slip (or taking out a loan) for $500 or more worth of flying model aircraft.

Fig. 1-7   A radio-control Pylon racer built from a Prather Products' "Quarter Midget" kit. *Courtesy Prather Products.*

Ready-Built Models

One of the major reasons why you buy a book like this one is the hope that the authors just might make some of your buying decisions for you. We can't blame you for hoping for a guide through the hobby of flying model aircraft, because it really is an extremely broad pastime that can demand anything from a dollar a week for lost hand-thrown balsa wood gliders to a $2000 investment in a quarter-scale radio-control aircraft that burns more expensive fuel than your car and more of it.

Our best advice is this: try to examine your reasons for wanting to get involved in the hobby. If you think you'd rather fly than build, for example, then start with one of the almost-ready-to-fly aircraft or one of the simple foam plastic kits that can be assembled in an evening. If you'd rather build, then start with something simple like one of the sheet balsa kits that require only an evening's worth of time to assemble, so you'll know for certain your efforts will result in a flying model aircraft. Far too many potential enthusiasts are lost because they felt they had to start out with the more expensive models or the most complex kit and they never got beyond the buy-it-for-the-shelf stage. Take a stronghold on your ego and buy one of the beginner models, even if you have to tell the hobby shop owner it's for your nephew's birthday.

If your reasons for wanting to become one of us include an overwhelming desire to make your own "bird" fly, then give radio-control sailplanes a chance. Free flight sounds simple but, once you get beyond that $1 sheet balsa wood glider stage into the "stick" models with fuses and dethermalizers, things get complicated. It really takes more skill and experience to build and fly free-flight models than radio-control sailplanes. You'll have to invest a bit more in obtaining a radio transmitter and receiver setup, but with them you'll learn to fly a lot quicker and much of your acquired knowledge can be applied to free-flight models later on. For that first aircraft pick one of the inexpensive sailplanes with illustrated plans and simplified construction that probably don't look much like any full-size glider. If you want one of the complex fiberglass and built-up balsa kits for that second aircraft model, you can always ask the hobby shop owner to have it built for that "nephew" of yours if you feel you lack the skill or patience to build it yourself.

We've tried to keep the models in this book as simple as we could and still show you the incredible range and variety the hobby offers. Less than one-percent of the available aircraft models are illustrated on these pages, and there are an equal number of plans available for those who want to build their own. There are thousands of different model aircraft available.

True-To-Life Scale Models

You'll find that we've included an entire chapter on scale models in this book, and you'll see photographs of what are most realistic scale model aircraft in almost every chapter. This is the time to give you one of the facts about flying model aircraft: Most scale models just don't fly as well as the full-size prototypes. There are two problems inherent in any truly accurate scale model: It's impossible to scale down the effect of gravity or the size of air molecules to match the scale of the model, and the air is far too dense for a scale-size airframe. With few exceptions, the models that look most like models fly much better than the models that look precisely like real airplanes. It is true that an experienced model aircraft flier can make most of those accurate scale models fly as well as many of the model-like aircraft, but you are still a long way from becoming an experienced flier. You'll find that even the "toy" models like the Cox-brand plastic ready-to-fly aircraft are marked "beginner", "intermediate", or "advanced".

The most important fact you can learn from this book is to select a beginner type model or at least a model that looks like a model for that first or second aircraft. When you've learned to fly with a model that's meant to fly like a model, then you can progress to a model that's meant to fly like the real thing. Master that stage, and you just might be ready for some of the free-flight competition models, the "R/C pattern" or "control-line stunt" planes, the "Pylon racers," and the helicopters that all actually fly far better than any full-size aircraft.

FEDERAL AERONAUTICS ADMINISTRATION
OPERATING STANDARDS FOR MODEL AIRCRAFT

1. *Purpose*

This advisory circular outlines safety standards for operators of model aircraft, and encourages voluntary compliance with these standards.

2. *Background*

Attention has been drawn to the increase in model aircraft operations, and the need for added caution in the case of free-flight and radio controlled types to avoid creating a noise nuisance or a potential hazard to full-scale aircraft and persons and property of the surface.

3. *Operating Standards*

Modelers, generally, are concerned about safety and do exercise good judgment when flying model aircraft. However, in the interest of avoiding undue criticism from affected communities and airspace users, compliance with the following standards is encouraged by operators of radio controlled and free-flight models.

    a. Exercise vigilance for full-scale aircraft (get other people to help if possible) so as not to create a collision hazard.

    b. Select an operating site at a sufficient distance from populated areas to avoid creating a noise problem or a potential hazard.

    c. Do not fly higher than 400 feet above the surface.

    d. Do not operate closer than three miles from the boundary of an airport unless permitted to do so by the appropriate air traffic control facility in case of an airport for which a control zone has been designated, or by the airport manager in the case of other airports.

    e. Do not hesitate to ask for assistance in complying with these guidelines at the airport traffic control tower, or air route traffic control center nearest the site of the proposed operations.

Fig. 1-8

OFFICIAL ACADEMY OF MODEL AERONAUTICS
SAFETY CODE

General

1. I will not fly my model aircraft in competition or in the presence of spectators until it has been proven to be airworthy by having been previously successfully flight tested.
2. I will not fly my model higher than approximately 400 feet within 3 miles of an airport without notifying the airport operator. I will give right of way to, and avoid flying in the proximity of full scale aircraft. Where necessary an observer shall be utilized to supervise flying to avoid having models fly in the proximity of full scale aircraft.
3. Where established, I will abide by the safety rules for the flying site I use, and I will not willfully and deliberately fly my models in a careless, reckless, and/or dangerous manner.

Radio Control

1. I will have completed a successful radio equipment ground range check before the first flight of a new or repaired model.
2. I will not fly my model aircraft in the presence of spectators until I become a qualified flyer, unless assisted by an experienced helper.
3. I will perform my initial turn after takeoff away from the pit, spectator, and parking areas, and I will not thereafter perform maneuvers, flights of any sort, or landing approaches over a pit, spectator, or parking area.

Free Flight

1. I will not launch my model aircraft unless at least 100 feet downwind of spectators and automobile parking.
2. I will not fly my model unless the launch area is clear of all persons except my mechanic and officials.
3. I will employ the use of an adequate device in flight to extinguish any fuses on the model after it has completed its function.

Control Line

1. I will subject my complete control system (including safety thong, where applicable) to an inspection and pull test prior to flying.
2. I will assure that my flying area is safely clear of all utility wires or poles.
3. I will assure that my flying area is safely clear of all non-essential participants and spectators before permitting my engine to be started.

Fig. 1-9

Chapter 2

▶ Basic Aerodynamics

Man's fascination with flight has led him to apply the natural laws of flight to a science that bears upon both full-size aircraft and models. You'll find it a whole lot easier to avoid crashing your model aircraft if you understand just what makes it fly and how the various control surfaces alter its course through the air. You may be surprised to learn, for example, that it's really not the wind but the aircraft's wing shape that keeps it in the air or that the speed of the propeller may be less important than its *shape*. There isn't room here to present even a short course in aircraft design for those who wish to create their own flying model aircraft. There are volumes much thicker than this one that deal with only the background information you'd need to create your own airplane. After you've mastered model aircraft flight with several different types of aircraft, from free-flight powered models to radio-control sailplanes, you'll have some idea of how different shapes can affect a model's performance. Learn to fly several different exact-scale model aircraft before you think you can just use a set of real airplane profiles or plans and scale them to fit a .20-to.60-cubic inch engine—it's often necessary to alter the shape of the wing's cross section (the airfoil) and/or to slightly enlarge the shape of the moving control surfaces to make a scale model fly well. We will try to give you the background information you need to understand why one model flies so much differently from another.

The Basic Principle

Flight is impossible without the expenditure of some form of energy. Even a hot-air balloon needs the energy to fuel the flame that heats the air; energy is needed to separate and purify the helium used for that type of lighter-than-air flight. The energy of the wind or of hot air rising is necessary to allow a fixed-wing aircraft or a bird (with stationary wings) to gain altitude. We're dealing with winged flight, so the type of energy that most concerns us is the type that keeps air moving over the wings of the aircraft. That energy can be the speed of the airframe through the surrounding air, the energy of warm rising air, or the force of gravity trying to pull the aircraft back to earth and thus forward in the aircraft's glide path. Most often, the energy that makes flight possible is a combination of two or more of these forces. A fifth type of energy for the flight of an airplane is that required to get a glider or sailplane off the ground and into the air so the wings can create lift and so that lift as well as the rising air currents can keep it aloft. That fifth type of energy may be the power of a hand launch, a runner with a towline, a "Hi-Start", or an electric winch system. Modelers seldom use a powered aircraft to pull a glider or sailplane into the air, but that's the most common way the prototypes are launched.

The aspect of the hobby/sport that makes it so much a sport of skill lies in making all five of these forces work most effectively for sustained flights or for precision maneuvers. You can make those forces work most effectively by precision assembly and correct alignment of a kit-built airplane and by the careful adjustment of the various control surfaces so they are most effective in producing a stable flight.

The Secret of the Birds

It took historic man thousands of years to uncover the secret of flight that birds possess. Ironically, the secret was right there in the obvious means of flight, the shape of the birds' wings. Man manipulated the cross sectional form of the birds' wings to better suit the hard surfaces of earlier wooden and later metal wings. The resulting modified teardrop shape is the familiar airfoil that is used, in one form or another, in the wings of every aircraft. The airfoil is a cross section of wing as it would appear if you were to cut through it in a direction going from the leading edge to the trailing edge. The shape of the wing when viewed from the top or bottom of the aircraft has a definite but subtle effect on the aircraft's flight performance. The fundamental principle behind the airfoil shape is that the curve over the top of the wing is theoretically of a greater radius than the curve of the bottom surface of the wing (we'll see why "theoretically" a bit later). When the wing is pushed through the air by some type of energy, air molecules are forced more rapidly over the top of the wing to create a "low pressure" area. This "bulge" in the flow of air creates a "lift" that does exactly that: It lifts the wing (and, of course, the rest of the aircraft) to help overcome the force of gravity.

The airfoil shape has a second advantage; it disturbs the flow of the air over the wing as little as is physically possible so the air doesn't "drag" on the wing to slow it down. Yes, bird's wings do have this same clever combination of gravity-fighting "lift" with minimal energy-absorbing "drag". The bird, however, can alter the cross sectional shape of its wings a bit to create even more lift by curving the top so much that the bottom (called an "undercambered airfoil") is actually concave. This produces even higher pressure beneath the wing (because there is already a slight cavity under the wing), and it increases the lift. The disadvantage of having the top curve so much is that it also increases the amount of "drag". If a bird (or an aircraft) is relying soley on the rising warm air currents in a "thermal" to gain altitude, then the amount of lift the wing

Fig. 2-1   A Craft-Air "Sailaire" sailplane being carried aloft by a thermal.

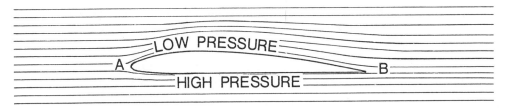

Fig. 2-2   The path of the air over a flat-bottomed airfoil from the leading edge (A) to the trailing edge (B). *Courtesy Estes Industries, Inc.*

shape provides can be extremely important. Some of the more advanced free-flight gliders have very pronounced differences in the top and bottom curves of the airfoil's cross sectional shapes in their wings and horizontal stabilizers to produce maximum lift at different air speeds.

If the aircraft does not have an abundance of power, the amount of drag that the airfoil shape can produce can be a real problem. The effect of the drag will be even more pronounced at the higher speeds that some aircraft reach in normal operation. For this reason, most jets and stunt planes (both full-size and model) have a symmetrical shape in the cross section their wings. This allows an absolute minimum amount of drag while the powerful engine produces more than enough energy for sustained speed, acceleration, and/or altitude gain. The symmetrical airfoil is important on a plane that is to be aerobatic because that type of aircraft is expected to fly as well upside down as it does right side up. The airfoil is generating "lift", relative to the aircraft, even when the aircraft (and the symmetrical airfoil-shaped wings) is flying inverted. An aircraft with a conventional airfoil (called a "flat-bottom airfoil") can be flown upside down for very brief periods during, for example, a loop or figure-eight aerobatic maneuver. The pilot or flier must, of course, be certain that the aircraft has enough altitude for the maneuver. He must also remember that the operation of the controls will be reversed during the moments of inverted flight.

Climbing High

When the aircraft's wings are forced through the air by the enrgy of gravity or by an engine-driven propeller, the airfoil shape generates a tremendous amount of "lift" due to the vacuum created on the upper surface of the wing and by the force of the air molecules striking the underside of the wing. This effect will exist even with a symmetrical airfoil wing cross section; that's the reason a stunt plane's wings or the wings of a pylon racer will still help it to gain altitude. Even the perfectly flat balsa wood wings of some of the inexpensive gliders and control-line kits will allow the aircraft to fly. The teardrop of "flat plate" wing shapes must, however, be accompanied with a reasonable amount of energy or power to sustain flight. The broad and relatively short wings of a stunt model or a "pattern" aircraft also reflect the fact that these types of models have an abundance of power, enough to pull such a large wing through the air.

The larger the surface area of the wing, the greater will be the "drag" of the wing as it passes through the air. If the wing area is too large for the aircraft's available power, the plane will respond sluggishly to the controls, and it may even be difficult to get it airborne. You can see examples of the other extreme of wing area versus power when you observe the long, thin wing sections and shapes of a sailplane or a free-flight model aircraft. The longer wings provide extra lift area, while the relatively thin wing width (called "wing cord") minimizes drag. When a model aircraft is flown at altitudes exceeding about 5,000 feet, a longer runway and a more powerful engine than that recommended by the manufacturer will be required for safe take-off and flight.

The angle that the wing strikes the airstream is called the "angle of attack". This angle can be adjusted by changing the angle of the stabilizer relative to the angle of the wing at the time the aircraft is designed or built. The flier of a control-line or a radio-control aircraft can also alter the angle of attack on the model during flight by moving the elevator controls to point the nose of the aircraft upward just enough to produce the desired amount of "lift". If the angle of attack is too great, the "lift" will be interrupted and the "drag" will become so great that the aircraft will stop flying momentarily; this is what is called the "stall angle". The aircraft may actually fall downward for a moment until (because of gravity) its nose is pulled down more than the tail. Once air speed is resumed, the components of lift, drag, and stability will once again combine for normal flight. If your model is flying in an area of gently rising air (in a "thermal"), it may actually gain altitude with its fuselage level with the horizon because the force of that rising air is producing an angle of attack that will allow increased lift.

Fig. 2-3   The path of air and the resulting forces when the angle of attack of an airfoil produces lift. *Courtesy Estes Industries, Inc.*

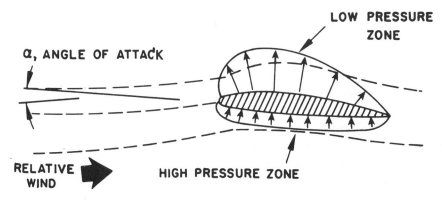

Fig. 2-4 Rising warm-air currents carry moisture that forms into cumulus clouds like these over the hills outside Reno.

In-Flight Stability

So far, we've been concerned mainly with how an aircraft flies in a straight-ahead attitude. There are a few other factors, besides the wings and their shape and the available energy sources (that keep the aircraft moving), that are important to prevent the aircraft from tumbling through the air like a broken tree limb. The vertical and horizontal control surfaces at the tail of the aircraft act like the feathers on an arrow or dart to keep the nose of the aircraft pointed in the direction of travel and to keep the angle of attack of the wings correct. The vertical surface at the tail is called a "rudder" and the horizontal surface is called a "stabilizer", even though both surfaces help to stabilize the aircraft's flight. Virtually any ready-to-fly or kit for a flying model aircraft is a stable design. You can, however, easily create an airplane model that is unstable if you try to design your own aircraft without a considerable amount of study and experimentation with aerodynamics. Each type of model aircraft is designed to be stable during the type of maneuvers that model is designed to fly. A pylon racer or control-line racer may be extremely stable in straight and level flight but only partly stable during maneuvers. An aerobatic or stunt plane will be stable regardless of which direction it is being flown (relative to the ground), but it may be rather sensitive to control in straight and level flight.

The "rudder" on virtually any aircraft has a teardrop or symmetrical airfoil shape, although a flat plate shape is sometimes seen on simple balsa wood models. This symmetrical shape ensures that the air passing over the rudder will have equal forces on both sides to give the aircraft right and left stability. The horizontal "stabilizer" on many early aircraft also had a symmetrical airfoil shape; however, some modern designs and many free-flight models have a stabilizer with a flat-bottom airfoil shape to produce a certain amount of "lift" at the rear of the aircraft during flight. In general, though, the shape of the airfoil on the horizontal stabilizer is designed to produce an air flow that will give the aircraft up and down stability.

An airplane is often maneuvered into positions where "up" and "down" become meaningless, so some special terms have been applied to describe its movements or stability about itself. The aircraft's movements to the right or left are called "yaw" or "directional stability". The aircraft's movements up or down are called "pitch" or "longitudinal stability". The aircraft can also move in a third dimension or plane when it leans ("banks") to the left or right. This movement on an axis through the aircraft's fuselage is called "roll" or "lateral stability". Most airplanes also have their wings angled upward at the ends (when viewed from the front or rear of the airplane). When the wings are angled upward the effect is called "dihedral". The dihedral helps to translate the "yaw" produced by the rudder movement into a banked turn. That extra lift on the "upper" wing turns the aircraft and keeps it from slipping through the air sideways like a skidding automobile. Again, stunt planes and other aerobatic aircraft that are expected to fly upside down as well as they do right side up will have zero degrees of dihedral or perfectly straight wings when viewed from the front or rear of the fuselage. They use ailerons to produce a banked or coordinated turn. The aircraft's "center of gravity"

Fig. 2-5   The "yaw", "pitch", and "roll" axes of any aircraft cross each other at the center of gravity. *Courtesy Estes Industries, Inc.*

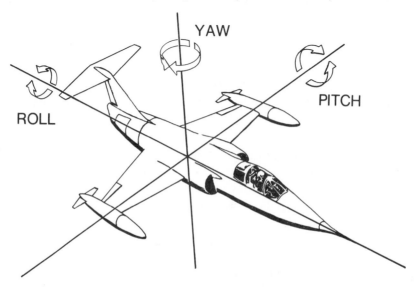

also has a rather profound effect on the stability during in-flight performance. If the plane were heavier on the left than on the right, it would tend to fall or bank toward the "heavy" side. You can sometimes increase the stability of a control-line model by adding just a bit of weight to the wing opposite the control lines, but there is an even greater force being effected by the control lines (and centrifugal force). If one wing of a radio-control aircraft model is heavier than the other, you'll have to adjust the controls constantly during flight to compensate for that offset center of gravity. In general, every effort must be made to be certain that the aircraft will balance if you hold a finger on the nose and another on the tip of the tail.

The center of gravity is the point where the roll, pitch, and yaw axis (lines) intersect. It's quite literally the pivot point for any movement that the aircraft makes while in flight, and it can have a pronounced effect on the aircraft's stability. The arrow or dart concept that we used to describe the importance of the rudder and stabilizer on the aircraft's stability applies equally to the center of gravity. Like the arrow or dart, an aircraft should have a center of gravity slightly forward so it is a little "nose heavy" for maximum stability in normal *level* flight. A full-size airplane, an airliner, or a speed-record aircraft should be designed for as much level stability as possible with (as is the case with the model) the center of gravity slightly forward. You can determine the center of gravity along the pitch axis by holding the aircraft with one finger on each of the wing tips. Move your two fingers forward toward the nose of the plane or back toward the tail until the plane will rock steadily and level between your fingertips. The correct center of gravity should be indicated on the plans; if not, then experiment with its location for best flying stability— try locating it about one-third of the wing chord back from the leading edge of the wing.

You can alter the center of gravity on any aircraft by simply adding some lead fishing weights or pieces of wire solder as close to the extreme nose or tail of the aircraft as possible. You may be able to replace the propeller's spinner with one that is a bit lighter or heavier, or you can add or remove a tail wheel or tail skid to alter the amount of weight on the nose or tail of the model without adding much excess weight. If the model is equipped with a radio-control receiver, batteries, and servo motors, you can make some drastic changes in the center of gravity by moving one or more of those radio components toward the front or rear of the fuselage. You may even be able to substitute lighter or heavier weight servo motors to help change the weight distribution and center of gravity. Do not even consider moving the wing's position on the fuselage to alter the center of gravity (unless you're a qualified aircraft design engineer), or you may destroy the model's in-flight stability.

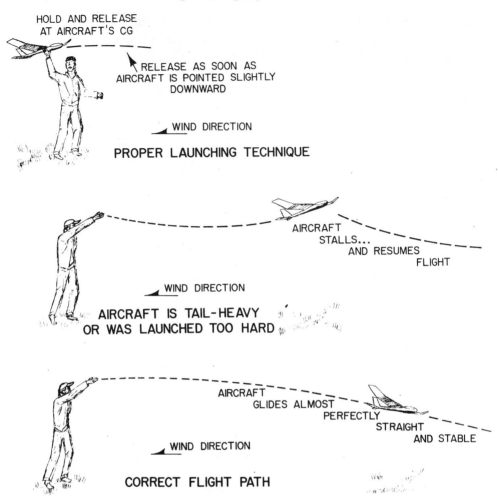

HOLD AND RELEASE
AT AIRCRAFT'S CG

RELEASE AS SOON AS
AIRCRAFT IS POINTED SLIGHTLY
DOWNWARD

WIND DIRECTION

PROPER LAUNCHING TECHNIQUE

AIRCRAFT
STALLS...
AND RESUMES
FLIGHT

WIND DIRECTION

AIRCRAFT IS TAIL-HEAVY
OR WAS LAUNCHED TOO HARD

AIRCRAFT
GLIDES ALMOST
PERFECTLY
STRAIGHT
AND STABLE

WIND DIRECTION

CORRECT FLIGHT PATH

Fig. 2-6   When the center of gravity is too far to the rear, the aircraft will stall (center). The correct path is shown at bottom.

Searching for CG

Almost any model aircraft, even a control-line stunt plane or a radio-control jet, should be stable enough to glide to the ground without engine power. A sailplane will, of course, travel much farther than a scale-model World War II fighter, because the fighter relies on its relatively heavy engine to sustain its air speed. A strong hand launch, from about shoulder level, with the model's nose aimed down *slightly* should provide enough power to keep any model aircraft from heading nose first into the ground. Some large radio-control and competition models are exceptions to this rule, but that's something for later. If you built the model according to the kit instructions, you should find that the wings are in perfect alignment with the horizontal stabilizer and that the rudder is perfectly vertical. The instructions may also suggest where the center of gravity point must be (actually the "pitch" axis is sometimes referred to as the "center of gravity") so you can add as much weight as needed to bring the model into the designer's specifications. You should also temporarily lock any controls that operate the movable elevator (on the rear of the stabilizer), the ailerons (on the rear of the wings), or the movable portion of the vertical stabilizer (the rudder) so the model will fly straight and level. Most control-line models have a rudder with a permanent right or left set, so you may have to do without a test glide to settle for a hand-held balance test for the center of gravity.

To test glide the model (to determine if its center of gravity is located correctly), give the model a healthy launch into the wind with the model's nose pointed just slightly downward. Hold the model as close to the center of gravity as possible when you release it. If the model glides to a smooth landing on its landing gear or skid, then the center of gravity is probably good enough for at least a few test flights. If the model dives down to land on its nose or propeller, then the center of gravity is probably too far forward, and some weight will have to be removed from the nose. If the model glides upward and stalls, then there is too much weight in the tail (center of gravity is too far to the rear), and you'll have to add some weight to the nose. It's also possible that you could have caused the model to stall during that test glide by throwing it too hard into the wind or by throwing it upward rather than slightly down; try it again to be sure, before you add or remove weight.

Complete Control

We have deliberately left until last the discussion of control surfaces that will allow you to alter the aircraft's movements in flight. Far too many modelers try to correct an aircraft model's apparent lack of stability by simply changing the position or angle of one of the movable surfaces. No airplane is going to fly efficiently in a maneuver if it is not stable in straight and level flight. The principles of flight we have discussed apply to the aircraft during virtually all stages of flight, regardless of where the ground or horizon may be. The control surfaces at the rear of the airplane that help provide most of its stability would, logically, be the ones to use to alter its course through the air, and that's generally just how it's done.

The term "rudder" applies to the entire vertical surface on the aircraft, including the movable or trimmable portion. The front of the vertical surface is sometimes called a "vertical stabilizer" to help avoid the confusion that arises when you are referring only to the non-movable portion of the vertical surface. When the rudder is pivoted left, the airflow over the surface is altered in a manner similar to the "angle of attack" we discussed relative to wings. The air pushes harder on the

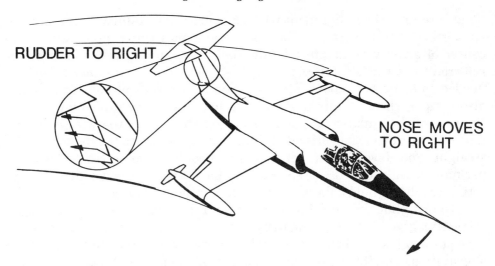

RUDDER TO RIGHT

NOSE MOVES TO RIGHT

Fig. 2-7 The movable control surface on the vertical stabilizer is called the "rudder". Right rudder produces a right turn. *Courtesy Estes Industries, Inc.*

protruding face of the rudder, and a partial vacuum is created on the opposite side to turn the aircraft effectively. Remember, though, that the actual pivot point is the "yaw" axis or the center of gravity.

The "elevator" is the movable surface on the horizontal stabilizer. That same "angle of attack" effect acts on the elevators to pivot the nose of the aircraft upward when the elevators are angled upward. The aircraft pivots downward when the elevator is pivoted into its downward position. The aircraft pivots up or down around its "pitch" axis (again, the center of gravity).

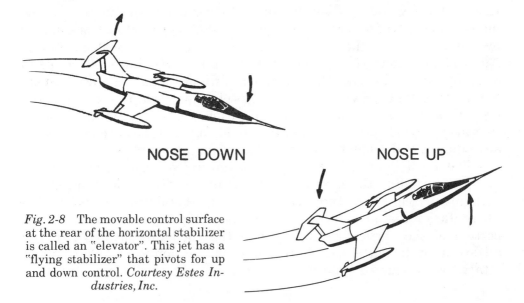

NOSE DOWN

NOSE UP

Fig. 2-8 The movable control surface at the rear of the horizontal stabilizer is called an "elevator". This jet has a "flying stabilizer" that pivots for up and down control. *Courtesy Estes Industries, Inc.*

AILERON UP - PRESSURE DEFLECTS
WING DOWNWARD

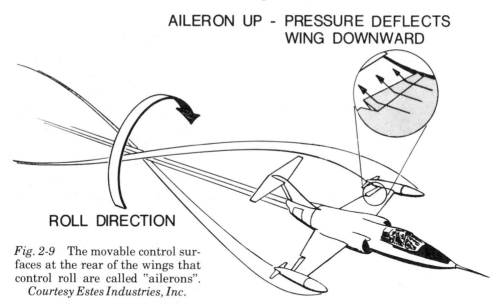

ROLL DIRECTION

Fig. 2-9 The movable control surfaces at the rear of the wings that
control roll are called "ailerons".
Courtesy Estes Industries, Inc.

An aircraft must be banked into a turn like a motorboat to keep the
airflow from sliding out over the wings as they move sideways through
the air. It is possible to turn an aircraft without banking it, but the speed
of the turn must be very slow. You can keep the speed down by either
flying at a relatively slow speed or by making the turn with an extremely
large pivot radius so that it is little more than a gently curving straight
flight. This type of turn is perfectly acceptable for a sailplane or a
free-flight model. When you are attempting to perform quick and clean
aerobatic maneuvers with a radio-control aerobatic glider or a powered
radio-control aircraft, you must use some type of banking turn to
duplicate the maneuvers of the real aircraft. Virtually every full-size
aircraft including full-size sailplanes, has some type of banking control for
the turns. Small control surfaces on the rear edges of the wings (the
ailerons) control the banking in either a turn or when flying straight. If
the plane is banked in straight flight and that "banking" is allowed to remain, the aircraft will roll over along what is appropriately called the
"roll" axis. Roll is often used to enter inverted flight with full-size aircraft,
and it is one of the maneuvers possible *only* with radio control on a model
aircraft. The ailerons work in pairs, with the left one going up while the
right one goes down (for a counterclockwise roll or bank) and the right one
going up while the left one goes down (for a clockwise roll or bank).

There are sometimes some additonal flaps or control surfaces on the
wings of both models and full-size aircraft. Many sailplanes, for instance,
have at least one movable control surface on the top of each wing. These
are "spoilers" that are flipped upward by one of the radio-control servos.
The spoilers are down for most of the flight's duration but, when the flier

is ready for the aircraft to descend, he or she will trigger the spoiler release mechanism so the spoilers are raised. This "spoils" the lift at the wing and allows the aircraft to lose altitude in a gentle and controllable manner. A "dethermalizer" on a free-flight aircraft may appear in a similar form of movable control surface (some free-flight models have spring-loaded horizontal stabilizers that flip up to act as dethermalizers). This type of dethermalizer is actuated by a fuse or timer. The dethermalizer on a free flight airplane will send it spiraling gently to the ground —without it, the aircraft may just disappear into the clouds.

Some full-size aircraft and a few exact-scale models may also have additional control surfaces along the the rear of the wing that serve as

FLIGHT TROUBLE-SHOOTING CHART

Trouble	Probable Cause	Remedy
Plane dives (nose down)	Nose-heavy	Remove nose weight or add tail weight
	Plane launched downwind (insufficient air speed)	Launch plane into wind
	Elevator bent down	Bend elevator up slightly
	Stabilizer warped	Steam stabilizer (or heat the "Monocote") and reshape it
Plane dives to right (or left)	Rudder bent	Bend rudder slightly in direction opposite of turn
	Wing warped	Steam wing (or heat the "Monocote") and reshape it
	Right (or left) wing too low	Reassemble wing correctly
	Engine canted to right (or left)	Add washers to shim engine to the right (or left)
Plane stalls and then dives	Tail-heavy	Remove tail weight or add nose weight
	Plane thrown upwards at launch	Launch plane straight out
	Plane launched too hard	Launch with less thrust
	Elevator (or aileron) bent up	Bend elevator (or aileron) down slightly
	Engine canted upward	Add washers to shim engine downward
Plane responds too quickly to controls	Control horns too short	Mount control rods further out on horn or use longer control horn
Plane refuses to gain altitude	Wrong propeller	Use propeller with more pitch or larger diameter
	Engine too small	Use large displacement engine
	Rear of wing elevated	Remove wing and mount properly
	Model is too heavy	Remove weight

Fig. 2-10

"landing flaps". These flaps are lowered to increase the lift of the wings so the aircraft's speed can be reduced. Landing flaps appear on the scale model Corsair aircraft in Chapter 5. Some dive bombers, like the German Stuka and the American Dauntless, have "dive brakes" that serve to help stabilize the aircraft and to prevent excessive speed during dive bombing attacks. These dive brake flaps are also located along the rear edges of the wings.

Lighter-Than-Air Paints and "Skins"

None of the flying models in this book really qualify as lighter-than-air craft: that category is left for hot-air balloons. A minimum amount of weight and the effect of the airflow over the aircraft are, however, important considerations. The weight of the model and the movement of the air over it are affected considerably by the finish you apply to the model's surface. Most full-size aircraft are covered with smooth metal riveted in place with "flush rivets" that are, indeed, flush with the surface. Few model aircraft have that smooth a surface when they are assembled. It is necessary to paint virtually any model's wood, paper, or cloth surface to help keep it smooth, clean, and unaffected by any fuel spillage. The alternative to paint is to use one of the plastic "skins" or coverings like Top Flite's "Super Monocote" or "Econocote," Pactra's "Solar Film", "Coverite", or Polk's "Wing Skin". The plastic material sold under most of these trade names is colored and super-smooth with little enough weight to be almost as light as any series of paint coats that would produce a similar finish. It takes several coats of sanding sealer paint, more coats of colored fuel-proof paint, and a final coat or two of clear fuel-proof paint to complete a truly smooth "painted" finish on most model aircraft. The plastic "skin" coverings are a one-coat (for one-color) job.

Chapter 3

✈ Power Plants

Natural and man-made flying machines require some type of energy to lift themselves into the air. The preceding chapter discussed the natural forces that help a bird or a properly designed aircraft fly; now it's time to find out how man's machines are used to help him fly. The engines used in flying model aircraft are generally two-stroke internal-combustion power-er plants, but electric motors, powered by on-board rechargeable ni-cad batteries are becoming increasingly popular. The two-stroke engines include both diesels and conventional engines with single and twin cylinders, and there is even a Wankel rotary combustion engine for larger aircraft models. The displacement of these engines ranges from tiny .020-cubic-inch for trainers and lightweight free-flight models all the way up to 2.5-cubic-inch engines for the larger quarter-scale radio-control aircraft. The catapult-style "Hi-Starts" and tow lines, with both surgical tube "rubber bands" and electric winches for power, also fall into the category of "engines" or power plants.

The Internal Combustion Engine

A model aircraft may provide the opportunity for your first intimate acquaintance with the internal-combustion engine. You might as well make friends with the power plant, because you'll be spending a lot of time with it if you choose to build and fly model aircraft with this type of engine. There's something far more charming than intimidating about a miniature engine that allows those who never touch the hood release on their automobile to be able to rebuild a model airplane engine blindfolded.

The two-stroke engine in a model airplane operates on the same principles as the two-stroke engine you may have in an off-road motorcy-cle, lawnmower, or chain saw. The fuel and air mixture is fed into the crankcase through some type of carburetor. The "carburetor" may be just a small passage or port beneath the tip of a needle valve with a knurled knob on a .020 or .049 engine. The air for these engines is simply drawn into the crankcase through a hole or port in the side of the cylinder. That same hole serves as an exhaust port when the piston is on its downward or "power stroke". A thin sheet metal or plastic "reed valve" is installed over the fuel inlet port inside the crankcase. The reed valve is spring-loaded to be closed until there is sufficient vacuum in the crankcase to pull it open

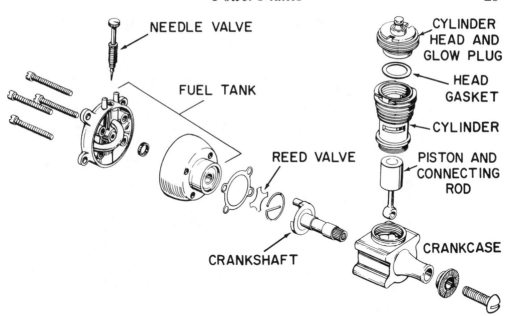

Fig. 3-1 The internal components of a typical two-stroke model aircraft engine (a Cox "Babe Bee" .049). *Courtesy Cox Hobbies.*

and, at the same time, to pull fuel past the needle valve from the fuel tank. The reed valve is pushed closed by its own spring pressure and by the force of the compression beneath the piston when the piston moves down the cylinder. The larger engines and engines intended for radio-control models usually have the carburetor mounted on the crankcase. The carburetor functions much like the one on your car to mix the proper quantities of fuel and air for any engine speed, and it has a throttle for speed control. The engine produces its power by igniting the mixture of fuel and air in the combustion chamber between the top of the piston (when the piston is at the top of its upward stroke) and the bottom of the cylinder head. The burning gases force the piston downward, and the crankshaft transfers that energy into the torque that turns the propeller.

Enough heat is generated by the compression of the fuel/air "gas" in the combustion chamber to keep the glow plug in the cylinder head red hot all the time the engine is running. The heat of the glow plug, combined with the heat of compression of the gases, ignites those same fuel/air gases. The burning gases expand almost instantly to force the piston back down the cylinder bore to create the "power stroke". The piston's travel back up the cylinder to pull the fresh fuel and air into the crankcase is called the "compression stroke". That expanding fuel/air gas is *not* really an explosion, just a rapid burning and release of energy; an explosion would blow a hole in the tip of the piston or blow the cylinder head off the engine. If you use the incorrect type of fuel for your model

STROKE 1: POWER, EXHAUST, FUEL TRANSFER

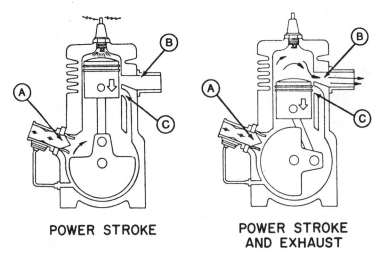

POWER STROKE

POWER STROKE
AND EXHAUST

A — REED VALVES
B — EXHAUST PORT
C — TRANSFER PORT

STROKE 2: COMPRESSION AND INTAKE

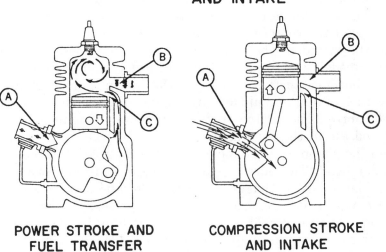

POWER STROKE AND
FUEL TRANSFER

COMPRESSION STROKE
AND INTAKE

Fig. 3-2　A cutaway view of the operation of a two-stroke engine. The crankshaft is rotating one turn clockwise. *Courtesy John Deere.*

aircraft engine, or decide to mix your own for more more power, you may very well cause just such an explosion in the combustion chamber!

The engines that have glow plugs that glow only when the engine is being started (or no glow plugs at all) are the only true "diesel" engines. That steadily glowing glow plug acts merely as a conventional type of ignition system that is "timed" by the compression of the fuel/air gases to ignite the mixture. In a true diesel, *only* the compression of the fuel/air gases is used to ignite these same gases. When the word "diesel" is added to the term "two-stroke", the type of engine that is being described has neither a spark plug nor a glow plug.

A simple "two-stroke" (no diesel) is an engine that usually has a spark plug that is ignited only once each time the piston moves upward. A distributor, magneto, or capacitive discharge system generates *and* times the spark so it will flash across the wires on the engine end of the spark plug to ignite the fuel/air mixture in the combustion chamber. The wires are large enough so that they do not glow; they spark *only* when "told" to do so by the engine's ignition system. That spark is timed to occur just before the piston reaches the top of its travel to gain the maximum amount of power from the burning fuel and air mixture. The Wankel rotary combustion engine operates on a similar principle to the two-stroke in that it has no valves (the four-stroke engines in most automobiles have at least two valves for each cylinder). The Wankel utilizes a triangular-shaped piston that tumbles around inside the cylinder to drive its crankshaft.

Starting Techniques

Almost every modeler has trouble starting the engine in a model aircraft, and the reason is almost always the same: a step was skipped somewhere along the way. A new engine often won't start without a dozen tries to get the glow plug working properly and enough fuel-soaked oil into all the cavities. Once the engine has been run once or twice, however, it should start with just two or three flicks of the propeller (or against the wind-up spring, if one is fitted). The "Engine Trouble-Shooting Chart" (Fig. 3-9) will tell you what to look for if there really is a problem; but go over the starting sequence carefully and systematically to find out where there was "pilot error" before you blame the machinery. Part of your responsibility in starting the engine lies in seeing that all the mechanical elements are functioning properly, and the "Engine Trouble-Shooting Chart" can be a help for that initial phase of starting any engine.

The first step in starting the engine is to fill the fuel tank with the correct fuel mixture for the engine you are using. The engine will include instructions on the selection of the proper fuel. When the tank is full, turn the needle valve in (clockwise) until you can just feel it bottom, then turn it out the number of turns specified in the instructions furnished with the engine. You may have to turn the needle valve back in a turn or two to

Fig. 3-3   Fill the fuel tank until you can see the fuel squirt out the breather hole in the fuel tank.

Fig. 3-4.   Connect a new battery to the glow plug with the special clip provided in most "starter" kits.

compensate for the lack of oxygen (you'll need less fuel because there's less air) at altitudes over 5,000 feet. Next, squirt a dozen drops of fuel into the open hole or port in the side of the cylinder while you turn the propeller over by hand. This will pull fuel into the crankcase and the cylinder head to "prime" the engine.

You'll have to work quickly, once the engine is primed, to take advantage of the available "extra" supply of fuel. Never connect the battery to the glow plug while you are adding fuel to the tank or priming the engine, because the fuel may catch fire. Most of the model airplane fuels burn with an invisible flame, so be extra careful! When the battery is connected, rotate the propeller against the return spring (if the engine has one) and give at least one full turn in the opposite direction to let the propeller spin to start the engine spinning a few turns. If the engine fires and begins to turn, adjust the needle valve to keep it running, remove the battery clip from the glow plug, and watch out for that spinning propeller! If the engine stops when the battery clip is removed, close the needle valve a half-turn and try it again. If the engine still fails to turn or start, go back to the beginning of the starting sequence and try again. If the engine is thoroughly flooded with liquid fuel, you can help clean it out by blowing through the cylinder ports while you slowly turn the propeller; when it's dry, try to start it again immediately without any additional priming.

Fig. 3-5 Many engines have a special coil spring starter. Hook the starter spring over the propeller.

Fig. 3-6 Hold the propeller against its starter spring until you are ready to start the engine, then release it.

Fig. 3-7 Hold the airplane with one hand while you adjust the needle valve screw with the other hand to obtain smooth engine operation.

Fig. 3-8 The K&B/Veco .19 engine (left) has a carburetor built into the crankcase. The K&B .21 engine (right) has a separate Perry brand carburetor.

If the engine has started, turn the needle valve to adjust the engine speed. Turning the valve in (clockwise) speeds up the engine, while turning it out (counterclockwise) slows the engine. You'll have to judge the engine speed by the sound, and you may kill the engine once or twice before you get the knack of adjusting its speed properly. The starting setting on the needle valve should produce a relatively slow engine speed with a rough, sputtering sound. Let the engine run for about 60 seconds to warm it up. It's actually hot enough to burn you, so be careful! When the engine is warm, slowly turn the needle valve IN and listen for the engine speed increase that should occur with each half-turn of the valve. When the engine reaches its peak and the next half-turn causes it to slow, you've gone far enough; now turn the needle valve back OUT a full turn to slow the engine a bit below its peak. The engine will then be running just a bit rich (too much fuel for the available air supply), but the mixture should be just right when the aircraft is in the air with the engine pulling its load.

Here's the tricky part of starting any engine: you won't ever be certain that those initial needle valve settings made before the engine started are correct. You may find that the engine starts running at almost its peak speed the first time it fires. The only way to be sure of what's happening is to learn to hear and feel the effect of turning the needle valve on the engine speed *and* to be aware of whether the engine is obviously getting far too much fuel. If it's getting too much, it will be spitting raw fuel out the ports in the cylinder while it is running. If a half-turn IN on the needle valve makes the engine run slower instead of faster, then you've gone beyond the optimum setting, and it's time to start turning the needle valve back out that single turn or less.

When it's time to restart a warm engine, a slightly different procedure must be followed: Refill the fuel tank. Open the needle valve one full turn beyond the setting where the engine was running. Do not add the "primer" fuel to the cylinder ports, because the hot cylinder might ignite the raw fuel! Go directly to the battery connection step, turn the propeller against its spring, start the engine, and disconnect the battery clip to the glow plug. The needle valve can now be turned back in a full turn to its correct running position.

ENGINE TROUBLE-SHOOTING CHART

Trouble	Probable Cause	Remedy
Engine won't start	Poor electrical connections	Clean glow plug and wire clip. Remove and install both wires to starting battery
	Weak battery	Use only a fresh lantern battery (not the "A"-size sold with some "starter sets")
	Cylinder head or glow plug loose	Tighten both with wrench supplied with engine
	Fuel line blocked or bent	Check and clean fuel line
	Burned-out glow plug	Remove head, connect battery to glow plug as you would to start, and see that wire inside glow plug really does have an orange glow
	Engine flooded	Close needle valve one turn
Engine runs for a short burst only	Engine needs more fuel	Open needle valve ½ turn and restart
		Check for a full fuel tank
		Check for a clogged or bent fuel line
Engine stiff or kicks back	Engine flooded to the point of being full of liquid fuel	Close needle valve and turn propeller until engine clears itself, then adjust needle valve and start again
Engine runs backward	Engine started without proper use of spring-loaded starting devise	Throw a rag into spinning propeller to stop engine and restart properly
Engine is low on power	See "Engine won't start" causes	Usually the same remedies that cure starting troubles will cure lack of power problems
	Propeller loose	Tighten propeller screw or nut
	Piston or cylinder worn	Have a dealer replace piston and cylinder or buy new engine
	Engine too small size of aircraft	Purchase a larger engine

Fig. 3-9

Selecting the Proper Fuel

Most model airplane engines are strong enough to withstand the use of special commercial blends of model airplane fuel intended for stunt or racing planes. A fuel with about 25-percent nitromethane (or less) is about as powerful a potion as you should use until you are completely familiar with the operation of both the airplane and its engine. The use of racing fuels may void the warranty on your engine, and prolonged use will very often burn out the glow plug. If you decide on racing fuel for more power, be sure to buy one or two spare glow plugs. The racing fuel may even be necessary to get some airplane/engine combinations to fly properly at altitudes above 5,000 feet. Cox "Flight Power", Fox "Missile Mist", and K&B "1000" are three examples of high-performance fuels that can increase the speed and power of your engine with a minimal chance of damage. These fuels increase the amount of heat the engine produces, and that extra heat can burn the glow plug wire through and cause severe damage to the working parts of the engine. A larger muffler will be needed, for most engines, if racing fuel is used. The all-out racing fuels, like Cox's "Racing Fuel" and K&B's "Speed Fuel", can burn out a glow plug every flight. Most model aircraft fliers would be better off to fit a larger engine than to use racing fuel. If you do decide to run racing fuels, you can minimize the deposits the special oils in the fuels leave by running a half-tank of regular fuel through the engine every other flight.

Fuel Tanks

Many of the .020-to-.049-cubic-inch displacement engines have a tank built right into the base of the engine. Most engines, however, require a separate fuel tank with a flexible fuel line connecting the tank and the engine. The optimum-size fuel tank should give a 5-to-12-minute flight. These sizes will give roughly that flight duration with "sports" type fuels: 2-ounce tank for a .10-cubic-inch (or smaller) displacement engine, 4-ounce tank for a .19 engine, 6-ounce for a .29 to .40 engine, 8-ounce for a .45-to-.50 engine, and 12-ounce for a .60 engine. The tank should be mounted so the centerline of the tank is a quarter of an inch below the centerline of the aperture where the fuel is injected into the carburetor (or, in the case of the smaller engines, where the fuel is fed directly to the crankcase, a quarter inch below the level of the fuel port).

The instructions furnished with most tanks describe how to install the fuel pickup line with a lead weight or "clunk" to keep the line at the bottom of the tank regardless of how the tank may be tilted or inverted. The fuel line may have to be reinforced, on larger tanks, with a piece of the next-larger diameter fuel line over the regular fuel line. The telescoping piece of fuel line must be just long enough to allow the line inside the fuel tank to move to any wall of the tank. The reinforced fuel line will then be stiff enough so it cannot bend back over itself or kink in a sudden maneuver or when landing.

Fig. 3-10 Bolt-on expansion chambers, like this one from RJL, can increase power and reduce exhaust noise on some engines.

Mufflers

Most model airplane engines are supplied with a muffler or at least a mounting area for one of the accessory mufflers and instructions on how to select the proper muffler to match the engine. The engine will produce a bit more power and a few hundred more revolutions per minute without a muffler, of course, but the price you pay for that extra bit of performance could very well be the right to fly model airplanes at all—it's against the law, in most cities, to fly an unmuffled airplane. You are also irritating the citizens who can force laws to be passed to ban *any* type of model airplane flying. If you need more power, then use a racing fuel, or simply buy the next-size-larger engine.

Choosing Engines and Propellers

The chart in Fig. 3-11 will give you the basic combinations of aircraft size and weight, engine size, and propeller diameter and pitch (the angle of the individual propeller blades) that work best for most types of aircraft. The chart is not the absolute law in any of these areas, but it will give you a place to start if you are not certain which combination to use. Don't try to outguess the manufacturer of your model airplane kit, however: if the manufacturer recommends a specific engine (and propeller), he probably has designed the entire model around that engine. An oversize engine can make the aircraft too nose-heavy, in spite of any extra power, so it will be unstable in flight. An oversize propeller or one with too much pitch can overload the engine and cause it to get so hot that it will weld itself together.

The best test for a proper propeller is to try it on the engine while you hold the aircraft stationary. If the engine cannot reach peak speed (with the needle valve temporarily turned in for that peak speed), the propeller is probably too large or has too much pitch for that engine. If the engine has the power to pull it, the greater the propeller's pitch, the faster the air speed. On the other hand, you may have to use a smaller pitch to provide enough power to get the aircraft through the grass at the flying field for take-off speed. The smaller pitch propellers are also one way to slow an aircraft down a bit while you learn to fly it.

Most ready-to-fly aircraft are fitted with propellers made from nylon or a similar flexible and strong plastic. The nylon propellers will withstand frequent nose-in landings without breaking, but they will fatigue to the point where their tips flex excessively. If you can see that the tips of the spinning propeller are moving more than a quarter-inch back and forth along the direction of the fuselage, the propeller should be replaced. Do not use any nylon propeller on an engine with a displacement larger than about .40 cubic inch. Wood propellers are more expensive than plastic ones and will break in a rough landing, but they are more efficient. Any wood or nylon propeller should be balanced by attaching it to a two-inch bolt the same diameter as the hole. Use a nut on each side of the propeller so about a half-inch of the bolt will stick out each side of the propeller. Let the ends of the bolt rest on your fingers so the end of the propeller is free to turn. Gently spin the propeller and mark the blade that stops in the down position. That blade is the heavy one, so sand or shave a few slivers off the face of it and repeat the process of spinning the prop until it coasts to a stop with a random order of which blade is at the bottom. There are several inexpensive commercial balancers that will make the job a bit easier than using the bolt and nuts.

Electric Power Plants

Electric motors may be the answer to the aircraft modeler's prayer for quiet flight. An electric-powered model aircraft is silent—and that is sometimes enough to allow it to be flown anywhere there's room to fly a kite. There are plenty of electric motors available with as much power and speed as two-stroke engines, and the electric motors may actually be lighter than engines with similar performance. The electric motors must, however, have onboard ni-cad rechargeable batteries for power; and the batteries do increase the total weight of the aircraft considerably. So far, the weight penalty of the batteries has limited the use of electric motors to models that are flown like free-flight aircraft; the electric motor is used to gain as much altitude as possible and the "energy" of gravity and air currents are used to perform aerobatic maneuvers or simply to prolong the duration of the flight. The electric motor and battery combination is light enough to allow the use of two- or three-channel radio-control on the aircraft. The lighter weight of two-channel radio receivers and the newer

SUGGESTED ENGINE AND PROPELLER SIZES

LIQUID FUEL ENGINES

Type and Size of Plane	Engine Size (cubic inches of displacement)	Propeller Size in Inches (diameter × pitch)
24- to 36-inch wingspan, 8- to 12-ounce total weight		
For free flight and radio control (e.g., Flyline's "Luton Minor")	.010 to .020	3 × 1½ 3 × 1¼ 4½ × 2
For control line and control-line stunt (e.g., Testors "Cosmic Wind")	.010 to .020	4½ × 3 4½ × 4½
36- to 60-inch wingspan, 12- to 16-ounce total weight		
For free-flight, radio-control powered sailplanes, and control-line aircraft	.020	4½ × 2 4½ × 3 4½ × 4½ 5 × 3 5 × 4
	.049 to .059	5½ × 4 6 × 2 6 × 3 6 × 4
	.061 to .100	7 × 3 7 × 4 7 × 6
36- to 60-inch wingspan, 16- to 48-ounces total weight		
For powered radio-control aircraft	.15 to .19	8 × 4 8 × 5 8 × 6
	.19 to .29	9 × 4 9 × 5 9 × 6 10 × 4 10 × 5 10 × 6
36- to 60-inch wingspan, 48- to 54-ounces total weight	.19 to .35	8 × 6 9 × 4 9 × 5 9 × 6 10 × 4 10 × 5 10 × 6
	.35 to .45	9 × 6 10 × 4 10 × 5 10 × 6 11 × 4

Type and Size of Plane	Engine Size (cubic inches of displacement)	Propeller Size in Inches (diameter × pitch)
		11 × 5
		11 × 6
60- to 72-inch wingspan,	.45	10 × 6
54- to 96-ounces total weight:	to	10 × 7
	.61	10 × 8
		11 × 5
		11 × 6
		11 × 7
		12 × 4
		12 × 5
		12 × 6

ELECTRIC MOTORS

Type and Size of Plane	Motor Size	Propeller Size in Inches (diameter pitch)
200- to- 300-square-inch wing area, 7- to- 15 ounces total weight	Astro Flight 020	5½ × 3 to 7 × 3½
250- to- 350-square-inch wing area, 15- to- 35 ounces total weight	Astro Flight 050	7 × 3½ to 6 × 4
300- to- 400-square-inch wing area, 15- to- 35 ounces total weight	Astro Flight 075	7 × 4 to 8 × 4
350- to 600-square-inch wing area, up to 42 ounces total weight	Astro Flight 10	8 × 4 to 7 × 4½
400- to- 600-square-inch wing area, up to 52 ounces total weight	Astro Flight 15	8 × 4 to 8 × 5
600- to- 800-square-inch wing area, up to 78 ounces total weight	Astro Flight 25	9 × 6
700- to- 800-square-inch wing area, up to 123 ounces total weight	Astro Flight 40	10 × 5

Notes for Both Engines and Motors

Engine size and/or propeller size or pitch must be increased at least one step for flying at altitudes exceeding 5,000 feet.

One step upward in propeller diameter is approximately equal to one step increase in propeller pitch (i.e.: a 5 × 3 and a 6 × 2 propeller should give almost equal performance). If the engine seems to lack the torque to turn a greater pitch, go to the next smaller pitch in the next larger diameter where possible.

These are only *suggested* engine (motor) and propeller sizes; if the engine seems sluggish or will not reach normal speed in flight without overheating, go to a smaller diameter and/or a smaller pitch. These sizes are based on near-sea-level tests with muffled engines.

Fig. 3-11

Fig. 3-12 The electric motor in this Cox "Electric Sportavia" is powered with a pack of eight rechargeable ni-cad batteries.

ultra-small servo motors is, of course, the best combination for the already rather heavy electric-powered aircraft models.

There are dozens of "one-evening assembly" foam plastic and simple balsa wood kits designed expressly for electric motors. The range includes both free-flight and radio-control aircraft of many full-size and model designs with both single and twin-engined (or-motored) types. Most free-flight power models and most radio-control models designed for fuel-powered engines can be converted to electric power with the use of the chart of "Suggested Engine & Propeller Sizes" (Fig. 3-11) under the "Electric Motor Size" heading. Astro Flight has numbered their electric motors (and most other brands use a similar system) to correspond with an equivalent fuel-burning engine's power and speed. The ni-cad rechargeable batteries do add between 4 and 35 ounces to the model's weight, depending on the size of the motor. That battery "load" will give a sustained full-power flight of about five-to-seven minutes. The dealers and manufacturers who sell motors usually can provide charts to suggest which sizes and types of ni-cad batteries are best for each of their motors.

The ni-cad (nickel and cadmium are the primary elements inside) batteries can be recharged in about 15 minutes with special chargers. The same firms that sell the motors offer the chargers. Most of them can also provide electronic speed controls for their motors if you do want to try three-or-more-channel radio control for reduced speed to prolong the duration of the flight. The motors can be bolted or clamped to the firewall, and their simple shape lends itself nicely to a totally hidden installation for exact-scale models. The motor and the battery pack must, however, receive some airflow; a quarter-square-inch area scoop and exhaust is enough for an Astro 10, a half-square-inch is required for an Astro 25, and proportionally larger or smaller scoops and exhaust holes for the other motor sizes.

Tow-Line Engines

The easiest way of launching a glider is simply to throw it into the air with a snapping action and full-body follow-through much like that used for pitching baseballs. When the sailplane has a four-foot wingspan, however, the hand-launch method isn't quite so practical. If you attach a 150-foot nylon tow line to a hook slightly ahead of the center of gravity with the opening toward the rear of the model, you can merely run along the ground into the wind and the aircraft will pull itself into the air. This is the way most of the "free-flight" outdoor competition models are launched. The radio-control sailplane people have an even better way.

The best way to launch a radio-control sailplane is to use one of the "mechanical" tow lines. The least expensive and best tow line for an individual is the rubber band style that is often called a "Hi-Start". This is

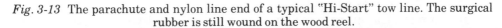

Fig. 3-13 The parachute and nylon line end of a typical "Hi-Start" tow line. The surgical rubber is still wound on the wood reel.

a 400-foot nylon monofilament line with another 100 feet of surgical rubber tubing with a stake to drive one end of the tow line into the ground and a loop on the other end to attach to the open-ended hook on the bottom of the model. The nylon line and surgical rubber tubing are tied together to form a single 500-foot tow line. The flier drives the stake into the ground and pulls his or her sailplane as far back against the tension (about 7-12 pounds for a glider with 72-to-100-inch wingspan) of the springy surgical rubber as possible. The sailplane is aimed into the wind with the stake end of the line directly upwind from the aircraft launch position. The flier then lets go of the aircraft, and the power of the rubber and the lift of the wings will carry the aircraft between 350 and 500 feet into the air. The radio transmitter can be used to adjust the wings' angle of attack to achieve maximum lift, and the rudder control will keep the model headed into the wind. When the model flies directly over the tow line's stake, the tow line loop will slip off the hook on the bottom of the fuselage. A small parachute is attached to the loop end of the tow line to allow the wind to help the hook disengage and to make it easier to find the end of the tow line on the ground. A spool or hand winch is often included to make it easier to store and unwind the tow line. The "Hi-Start" tow lines are available with heavy, medium, and light rubber for aircraft in the 16-to-40-ounce, 40-to-80-ounce, and over-80-ounce categories. The Cox "Launch Pail" and Astro Flight "Astro Start" are two examples of the typical "Hi-Start" tow line setups.

If you have the money or can form a club to pool your resources, the electric launching winch like the one sold by Hi-Flight Products is the

Fig. 3-14. The Hi-Flight Model Products' electric winch (top) uses a foot treadle speed control (right) with a bicycle hub (left) pulley.

most efficient way of getting a radio-control sailplane into the air. The electric winch is driven by a 12-volt electric motor like an automobile starter motor with a 12-volt automobile battery for power. The actual tow line is twice the length of a rubber band-style "Hi-Start", because the winch is located beside the flier, with the tow line extending out across the ground at least 500 feet (the distance can be as great as 1000 feet if you have the room). A pulley (actually a bicycle hub with ball bearings) is secured firmly to the ground, and the tow line goes back to the flier to hook onto the sailplane. The flier controls the action of the winch drum on the end of the electric motor shaft with a three-speed foot treadle. The flier hooks the tow line onto the sailplane and presses the foot treadle until the tow line is taut, then launches the model overhand into the wind while, at the same time pressing on the foot treadle so the tow line pulls the model aloft with the wing's aerodynamic "lift" carrying upward as the cable is reeled in. With practice, the flier can maneuver the sailplane's elevators by radio control plus the speed the winch is pulling in the tow line to send the sailplane upward at 45-degree angle to a height of about 500 feet or more. The complete rig sells for less than $200 plus the price of the storage battery. Most clubs mount the battery and motor/cable drum in a sturdy box to keep the mechanism clean and protect it during transit. It's the very best way to get a radio-control sailplane into the air in a hurry.

Fig. 3-15 The sailplane is launched with the flier's foot on the speed control treadle. A friend is holding the radio transmitter for this flier.

Fig. 3-16   The electric winch pulls in the tow line at precisely the rate of speed the flier
desires to allow maximum lift and altitude.

Chapter 4

Fly-by-Wire

More control-line model airplanes are sold then those in any other single category. The primary reason for the popularity of this segment of flying model aircraft is price; you can get a powered, remote-control, flying model aircraft into the air for between $15 and $25. The major disadvantage of the control-line flying (also called "U-control" flying) is that the aircraft is always flying in some type of circle around you. That's not such a bad thing, if you think about it, because it keeps the aircraft well within sight and not all that much closer than you might fly a "trainer" type radio-control model. For an experienced flier, the flight area is not really confined to a circle, but to a dome, or hemisphere with an altitude directly over the flier's head as great as the length of the control lines. Stunt planes can do anything around the periphery of that dome, and even a $15 ready-to-fly can do some aerobatic stunts, including "wing overs" with a path directly overhead. Control-line models, then, have a "universe" almost the same shape as that for a radio-control or free-flight model, the only difference being that the edges of that control-line "universe" are well within the sight of the flier.

The Flight Line School

There is only one control for most control line aircraft; the up and down movement of the elevators on the stabilizer. The rudder is set so the aircraft will always pull away from the flier (to help keep the control lines taut). The engine is set to run at full throttle, but the aircraft's speed will vary considerably, depending on the prevailing wind speed and whether the model is climbing or diving. Some of the more experienced modelers fit a third control line to regulate the throttle to adjust engine speed, but that's something to save for your fourth or fifth control line model. The two control lines are rigged so the aircraft will climb when you pull back on the hand lever to move the upper line toward you. The model will dive when you pull the lower line toward you with the control lever.

You cannot make any adjustments to the model aircraft or to the controls after the model is flying, so it's most important that you get everything right before takeoff. The engine should be completely broken in before you fly the model. You can break the engine in by running two or three tankfuls of fuel through it (letting it run long enough to consume

47

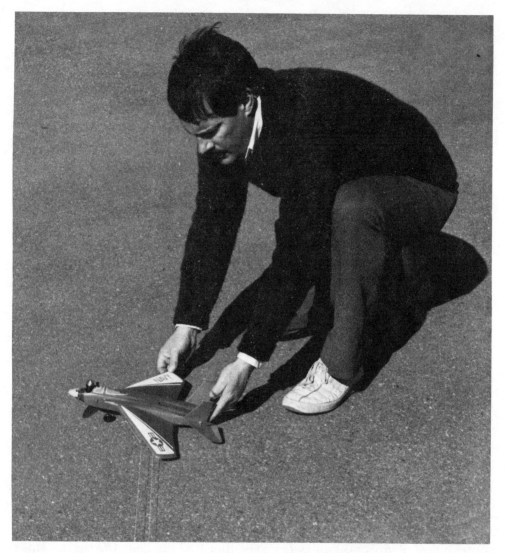

Fig. 4-1   Have a helper hold the model, with its engine running, while you hold the
control handle for takeoff.

each tankful). Adjust the needle valve, as described in Chapter 2, so the
engine runs at least a half-turn below the setting for peak engine speed.
This will make the fuel/air mixture a bit rich for on-the-ground operation,
but that should provide the extra fuel (and the extra oil that's mixed in
with the fuel) to keep the moving parts well lubricated and cooled. Be
certain, of course, that the propeller is on for these break-in periods. It is
most important that the needle valve be adjusted for peak engine speed
minus a half-turn every time the engine is started. The exact setting will
change, as the engine loosens up and the surfaces begin to wear in. You
may even have to adjust the needle valve while the engine is running

through those break-in periods. Adjust the control lines on the control-line handle so the handle is perfectly vertical when the elevator on the aircraft is in its neutral or level flight position.

Do not expect your control-line model to perform any type of stunt the first few times you fly it. The secret of real control, with control-line flying, is to keep every movement slow and deliberate with the same kind of care you'd take when walking on ice. Hold your arm straight and firm at the elbow and wrist so you can actually sight down your arm and straight on across the top control line to the aircraft. The movement of the control handle should come from the up-and-down movement of your entire hand and arm, pivoting *at your shoulder!* After at least a hundred flights, you'll begin to have enough experience to know when a very slight amount of wrist movement can be added to that arm and shoulder pivot for some of the very quick and sudden aerobatic maneuvers.

Your First Solo

Have a helper hold the aircraft while you get ready for takeoff. When you're certain the controls are working properly and that the engine is running properly, point toward the right to signal your flight crew to

Fig. 4-2   Adjust the length of the control lines so you can hold the control handle vertical, with the elevator horizontal and both lines taut.

release the model. Circle the flying field three or four times to gain those first three or four feet of altitude. Let the model decide when to takeoff even if it takes 25-to-30 feet to gain enough speed. If you find you must move the elevator, try raising your arm only about an inch and give the model a lap to see what its responses may be. If you can fly through an entire tank of fuel without allowing the model to change altitude more than an inch at a time, your first solo flight is a success.

When the model runs out of fuel, it will glide to the ground on its own if you follow it down by sighting quickly along your arm. Try to keep the control handle as near vertical as possible so the elevator will remain in the neutral or level flight position. The aircraft's reduced flying speed will automatically decrease the "lift" generated by the wings, so it will loose altitude without any correction in the controls. You may have to take several steps backward to keep the control lines taut as the aircraft's speed decreases.

The wind can be the greatest enemy the control-line modeler faces. It's impossible to take off or land directly into the wind, because you're flying in a circle. The solution should be obvious; never fly when the wind speed is any greater than five or ten miles an hour. If you are going to make a change in the elevator's position, do so when the model is flying across the wind so the aircraft can respond and stabilize itself before you come around and head into the wind. When you do make any change in the angle of the elevator, remember to return the control handle to the vertical position immediately before the aircraft has time to make a complete loop out of a simple change in altitude.

Keep any movement of the control handle very slight, and do it from the shoulder. The majority of crashes with control-line models are caused by too much elevator movement and too sudden overcorrection for that first mistake. Remember, you're flying close to the ground, so you don't have a lot of altitude to serve as a "safety zone" between the model and certain disaster.

The Model Aerodrome

The choice of flying site can make the whole sport more enjoyable. Try to find a place where you can take off and land on a hard surface like asphalt or concrete with about half to two-thirds of the area covered with grass about two inches high to provide some padding for those unplanned landings or crashes. If you have to choose, pick pavement and keep reminding yourself how important those slow changes in elevator position can be. Try to avoid tall grass that can tangle in the propeller and dirt that can find its way into the engine and the control lever and elevator hinges and pivots. Pick a site where the wind is the same at ground level and all the way to about 50 feet elevation. An open field or parking lot with no bushes or walls to partly block the wind is about the best flying

Fig. 4-3 *(left)* Hold the control handle vertical and straight in front of you with your arm and elbow straight during normal level flight.

Fig. 4-4 *(below, left)* Move your entire arm down slightly, without moving your wrist, to cause the aircraft to dive. (The elevator angle is exaggerated here.)

Fig. 4-5 *(right)* Move your entire arm up slightly, without moving your wrist, to cause the aircraft to climb.

site. You'll need an area almost a hundred feet in diameter to give yourself a little room to move around in the center of the circle and to allow the use of longer control lines after you gain experience.

Control Lines

The ready-to-fly airplanes like Cox and Testors in the "beginner" class can be flown in a circle as small as 15 feet in diameter. That's a good place to start until you get the feel of keeping the control lines taut. These "beginner" models can be flown in circles as large as a 25-foot radius after you've mastered full control with the smaller circle. The smaller balsa wood "Beginners" or "Trainers" kits and the Cox type of ready-to-fly models with .049-cubic-inch ("Half A") engines will perform nicely with 25-to-30-foot-long control lines even during "stunt" type maneuvers. The competition events for these small aircraft use control lines as long as 60 feet, but those models generally have larger engines and, therefore, much faster flying speeds. Control-line models with larger displacement engines can fly nicely with 60-to-70-foot control lines, but you can learn to control them a bit easier with 30-foot lines. Try increasing the lengths of the lines about 5 feet at a time, so you'll become familiar with the model's response to the controls and to the wind with the longer lines with no totally unexpected changes.

Fig. 4-6   Try to select a flying site that has at least a small area of hard dirt for a landing and takeoff strip.

Most ready-to-fly models are supplied with braided nylon strings for control lines. For aerobatic or stunt maneuvers, you should replace these lines with .008-inch multi-strand steel lines. Models with engines between .051- and .15-cubic-inch displacement should be flown with .012-inch multi-strand steel lines, and models with engines up to .36-cubic-inch should have braided steel lines .018 inch or larger in diameter. If you fit the steel lines, then fit solid-steel "piano wire" leadouts from the bell crank lever inside the model to about an inch past the tip of the wings. These wires should be about twice as large in diameter as the recommended braided steel wire sizes. Bend loops and wrap the steel wire around itself off the ends of the wings. Hobby dealers sell special clips for the quick attachment of the braided steel control lines to those solid-steel "leadout" lines. Be extra careful when using the braided steel lines to avoid flying anywhere near telephone or high-tension wires, because the current from the high-tension lines can actually jump through the air for dozens of feet to reach those steel control lines. Check the control lines *every* time you fly to see that they are not kinked or frayed at the knots.

Stepping Up

You'll soon know if you're going to "take to" control-line model aircraft as a sport. If you can master the controls and keep the lines taut, you'll soon be ready for "wingovers", loops, figure eights, and other "stunt" maneuvers. Most of the basic maneuvers illustrated in Chapter 12 for competition flying are based on the simple basic patterns shown in this chapter. Unfortunately, very few of the plastic ready-to-fly models are capable of inverted flight. Your first "step-up" should be the purchase of a propeller with more pitch to increase the speed of your existing model so it can at least climb straight up for the beginning of a loop or wingover. In time, though, you'll reach the full performance potential of your first aircraft and desire something with a bit more aerobatic performance. Several kits will accept the .049 engine from the Cox almost-ready-to-fly aircraft if you add the Cox bolt-on fuel tank to the rear of the engine. The Testors .049 engines must be fitted to a special bulkhead that is not included in any kit. Testors offers a set of plans for their own "Ambush" that can be made from sheet balsa and plywood, but even that model will not accept the engine from the Testors ready-to-fly planes. The "Ambush" is designed for the .049 Testors "8000" engine with integral fuel tank or for the similar Cox .049 engines. If you don't want to build from a kit or from balsa wood and plans, your choice of a second control-line model might well be a simple almost-ready-to-fly kit like the Cox "Super Stunter" with a molded plastic fuselage and tail and foam plastic wings. This model can be assembled in about an hour.

Don't be scared by the fact that a model is a "kit". The models with a solid sheet of balsa for the fuselage and similar flat sheets (but thinner)

Fig. 4-7   The plans for Testor's "Ambush" specify all the materials. It's a nice "second" aircraft. *Photo courtesy the Testor Corporation.*

Fig. 4-8   The Sig "Buster" is a "profile" type of "trainer" balsa wood kit that can be assembled and painted in a single evening. *Photo courtesy Sig Manufacturing Co.*

Fig. 4-9 The fuselage on the Carl Goldberg No. G25 "Flying Tiger" kit is a sheet of balsa, but the wing has a true airfoil with ailerons. *Courtesy Carl Goldberg Models, Inc.*

Fig. 4-10 This P-51 Mustang kit, from Sig, has modified proportions so it will fly better as a model than the real thing. *Courtesy Sig Manufacturing Co.*

Fig. 4-11   This Sig "Smith Miniplane" can be assembled as either a radio-control "sport scale" or a control-line "scale" model. *Courtesy Sig Manufacturing Co.*

for the wings, rudder, and stabilizer can be assembled by most 10-year-olds in two to three hours. The assembly techniques using cyanoacrylate cements like "Hot Stuff" and baking soda that are described in Chapter 9 allow you to assemble the model almost as quickly as you can push the parts together. The surfaces need only a light five-minute sanding to round the leading edges and to remove any rough spots. Spray cans of fuel-proof colored and clear paint make finishing just about as easy. You'll have to wait overnight for the paint to dry, but that's the only delay in the "three-hour" completion time. If you want to do some building, similar kits are available with the balsa wing spar and rib construction and tissue or, better, "Super Monocote" plastic covering. The very best stunt aircraft usually have flat balsa fuselages (called "profile") and balsa and spruce wings for maximum strength under the extreme "g" loads (several times the effect of gravity) that true competition aircraft models must withstand during their maneuvers.

Simple Stunts

If you own an aircraft with plenty of power (with an .049 or larger engine) and symmetrical wings that will allow inverted flight, you have the basic equipment to be a model aircraft stunt flier. The main missing ingredient is the skill that stunts require. Stunts must be learned a step at a time, if you expect to avoid crashing. First, know your aircraft well enough to be able to fly it perfectly level at about a 4-to-6-foot height.

Your first aerobatic or stunt maneuver should be a "partial wing-over". When the model is at a right angle to the wind, move your arm up

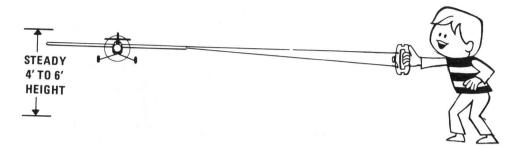

Fig. 4-12   Learn to fly at a 4-to-6-foot elevation with complete control regardless of slight wind gusts. *Courtesy Cox Hobbies.*

smoothly to make the model climb sharply at about a 25-to-30-degree angle. Bring your arm back straight while the model flies higher for half of the circle. When it comes on around and heads for the ground, pull it out of its shallow dive with the same movement you used to send it upward. That second movement should bring the model back to the same level it was on the opposite side of the circle when you started the maneuver. Practice this one until you can do the "partial wingover" for precisely half the circle with the model beginning and ending the maneuver at precisely the same altitude. Precise control is what stunt flying and combat maneuvers are all about.

When you get that shallow "partial wingover" down pat, try it with the half-circle flight at about a 45-degree angle to the ground. When that maneuver is perfected, increase the angle on each try until you are flying the model directly overhead in a true 90-degree vertical wingover. You'll learn faster and have more precision if you fly level for a few laps to regain your confidence and equilibrium. Putting several stunts back-to-back in a sequence is something for the experts; for now, you want to learn to control the aircraft with complete confidence.

Fig. 4-13   The "Partial Wingover" is the first stunt-flying maneuver. The length of the control lines is shortened in these views. *Courtesy Cox Hobbies.*

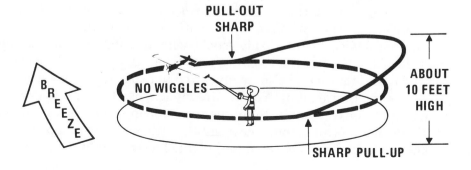

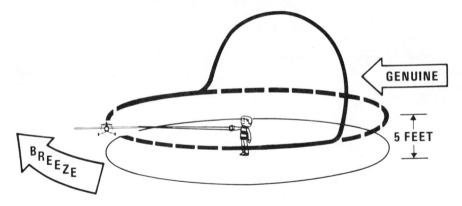

Fig. 4-14   Make the upward portion of the partial wingover
steeper and steeper until it is truly vertical; a "wingover".
Courtesy Cox Hobbies.

The inside loop is one of the basic stunt maneuvers. Many of the more complex patterns are based on the control perfection you learn with this fundamental. This one isn't accomplished by just setting the elevator at "hard up" and hoping; you'll need a gentle upward path to bring the aircraft into the loop and out of it. The top of the loop must be a bit tighter to help the plane maintain as much of its speed as possible during the critical transition from normal to inverted flight. This is the time to begin thinking as though you really were inside the aircraft, so you won't become disoriented and move the control handle in the opposite direction from the one you want. You can move your arm and hand in a miniature duplicate of any aerobatic maneuver to help maintain that "pilot/cockpit" image. Keep the control handle vertical, however, for the entire "inside loop" maneuver, including the brief inverted portion of the flight. Your first loops should be accomplished with just the barest amount of elevator angle so that the loop is very large, large enough for the aircraft to be almost directly over your head at the peak of the loop. With practice, you can make the loops tighter and tighter until they really do follow the same path as the model in Figure 4-15.

If you try to do several loops with a control-line model aircraft, you're going to end up with the control lines so twisted around each other that they can no longer move the bell crank lever inside the model. The secret of any aerobatic "pattern" maneuvers with a control-line model is to match any clockwise loop ("inside loop") with a counterclockwise loop ("outside loop") so the twisted lines are untwisted. One way to do this is to perfect the basic "figure eight" maneuver and to learn as many variations as you can of the figure eight. You've already learned the first loop of the figure eight; the next lesson is to fly the second loop, which is an "outside loop". Keep the control handle horizontal, with your palm up, for the entire outside loop portion of the figure eight. The second leg of the figure

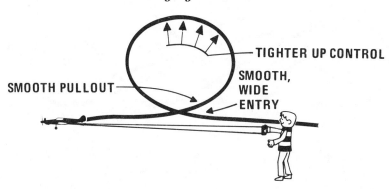

Fig. 4-15 Gradually tighten the diameter of the "inside loop" as you gain confidence and experience. *Courtesy Cox Hobbies.*

eight is flown with the model upside down or inverted. Inverted flight requires just the opposite control action of normal level flight. The "up" or "inside loop" is flown with the control handle as shown in Figure 4-16. Keeping the control handle near the vertical rudder angle will help you to orient yourself to the model's cockpit. You won't be able to turn your wrist or arm anywhere near 180 degrees without moving the control enough to crash the model. You must settle for about a 90-degree arm twist to control the aircraft while it is flying in the inverted position. If the inverted portion of the flight is going to be prolonged, you may find it easier to reposition the control handle back to vertical to match the upside down (relative to the control handle) rudder.

You can perfect your inverted flying technique by lengthening the amount of time the model spends in the inverted (left to right) portion of the figure eight. Your first few dozen figure eight maneuvers should be relatively tight, as shown at the far left (1) of Figure 4-17. Gradually

Fig. 4-16 Hold the control handle in the positions shown, while you follow the aircraft's path with your entire arm. *Courtesy Cox Hobbies.*

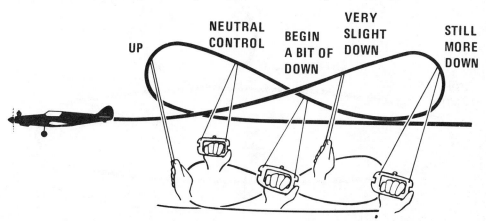

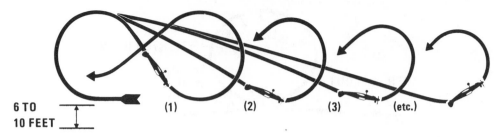

6 TO
10 FEET

(1)   (2)   (3)   (etc.)

Fig. 4-17 Gradually lengthen the inverted portion of the figure eight (1 through 3) to learn how to fly inverted. *Courtesy Cox Hobbies.*

increase the length of the upside down portion (2) and (3) as you gain confidence. If you feel the upside down or inverted flight is too disorienting, for now, then go back to some level flight and some tight figure eights until you gain more confidence.

The "outside loop" or counterclockwise loop is far more difficult. Many fliers find that an outside loop is much easier to accomplish if they keep the control handle in horizontal (rather then vertical) position from the time the model begins its vertical upward flight on through the top of the loop and into the vertical dive. When the model pulls back around the bottom of the loop, you can swing the control handle back to the vertical handle position. You may find more control with this palm-up position for outside loops (Fig. 4-18) and with a strictly vertical control handle position for the *entire* "inside loops" (Fig. 4-15).

Fig. 4-18 The "outside loop" begins and ends with the aircraft flying inverted. Keep a minimum 6-to-10-foot altitude. *Courtesy Cox Hobbies.*

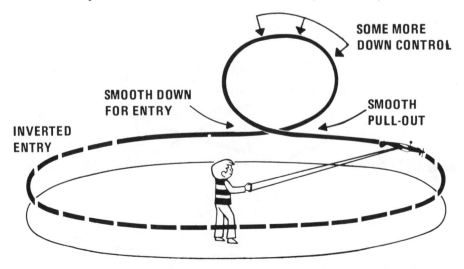

SOME MORE
DOWN CONTROL

SMOOTH DOWN
FOR ENTRY

SMOOTH
PULL-OUT

INVERTED
ENTRY

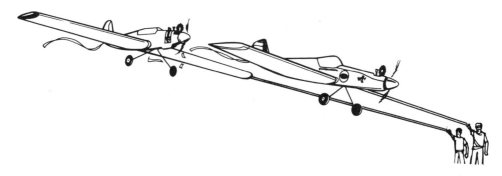

Fig. 4-19   When you are an experienced "stunt" flier, you might test your ability by flying
with another person in mock combat. *Courtesy Cox Hobbies.*

Combat

Two types of flying activities are available for control-line stunt fliers. One is the precision "pattern" flight contests with the full hemisphere of patterns around and above the flier as shown in Chapter 12. If you really love a perfect figure eight, then you might want to learn more complex patterns. The most exciting type of stunt flying, however, is the "combat" type of flying where two people stand in the center of the flying circle with their aircraft on exactly the same length control lines. Each model has a 10-foot-long strip of crepe paper tied to a 6-foot string from the center of the fuselage. The object of the "combat" is to chop your opponent's crepe paper to bits before he can do the same to yours or, better yet, chop through your opponent's string to score an immediate "kill" victory. The combat flights are for five minutes and, if there is no kill, the aircraft with the longest amount of crepe paper is the victor. The AMA has several classes of special combat competition for highly specialized models, but the thrills are the same with a .049-cubic-inch engine in a simple "trainer" or "stunt" model made from one of the simple sheet balsa wood kits. The AMA combat classes include competition for models with up to .36-cubic-inch engines. These planes fly and maneuver so fast that special pressurized tanks are needed to maintain the fuel supply. Crashes are so frequent that a contestant may bring as many as a dozen duplicate aircraft to one event. With the .049 combat, you won't have quite the number of crashes, but do use steel control lines and bring along plenty of spare propellers.

Chapter 5

Radio Control

There is no aerobatic maneuver that cannot be duplicated by an experienced flier "piloting" a scale-model aircraft by remote control. In fact, the models can often accomplish maneuvers that are impossible with real aircraft because the models are sometimes stronger and more powerful (for their size) than a full-size aircraft. Besides, there's no pilot in there to have to contend with the 10-g (ten-times the force of gravity!) loads that are a matter of course on many model aircraft aerobatic flights. It helps, too, when the "pilot" knows he's risking only a machine on a mistake, not a life. That's one of the reasons why radio-control helicopters can actually fly upside down for prolonged periods of time. You can truly fly like a bird with a peaceful radio-control sailplane, using the winds blowing up hillsides and the rising warm air currents called "thermals" to gain altitude as rapidly as a bird on the same flight path. The almost-magic of radio control, coupled with the newer and more sophisticated models that radio control has allowed, have made the newest model aircraft truly incredible performers. R/C, as radio-control is called, is the "can-do" corner of the hobby; if there's any type of full-size aircraft you admire, you can match its shape and probably better its performance with a flying R/C model.

Radios

The radio transmitter portion of a radio-control model aircraft system transmits low-frequency radio signals through the air to a receiver inside the aircraft. Small rechargeable ni-cad batteries provide more than ample power for the low-current draw of the transmitter and receiver. Control sticks or levers on the transmitter are moved to send a radio signal to the receiver. The more expensive "fully proportional" (sometimes called "digital proportional") systems are designed to provide almost perfect response in the aircraft; the further you push the lever on the transmitter, the more the receiver in the aircraft will respond. The receiver, in turn, sends an electrical signal to one or more tiny electric motors inside the aircraft. These motors are called "servo motors", or simply "servos," because they function only as servants to the receiver's signals. Today's sophisticated receivers translate the signals from the transmitter so that the servo motor will turn only in direct proportion to the amount the lever

Fig. 5-1   A simple-to-build Ace R/C "Mach None" radio-control model has a .049-cubic-inch engine. *Courtesy Ace R/C, Inc.*

on the transmitter is moved. A small wheel with holes near its rim is mounted on the servo motor shaft. The control rods (called "pushrods") that move the aircraft's control surfaces (and its throttle control) are pivoted from those holes in the servo wheel. The servo wheel rotates to move the pushrod, which in turn, moves the control horn on the elevator, rudder, or ailerons. The fully proportional types of radio-control transmitters and receivers normally provide linear response from lever to control surface. This means that if you move the control lever a little, the control surface moves a little; move the lever very quickly, and the control surface moves very quickly. The amount of movement and the speed of that movement are what a "fully proportional" radio-control transmitter and receiver offer to allow the flier total control over his or her aircraft.

Some pulse proportional radio-control systems, like those sold by Ace R/C, offer a form of inexpensive radio-control. The pulse proportional systems are updated versions of some of the very early types of radio-control systems in which the model's control surfaces actually flutter or "pulse" while the model is flying. The pulse, however, doesn't slow the model, because it happens too quickly for the air currents to be much affected. The primary advantage of the pulse proportional systems is that they are light enough to be used in smaller aircraft with .020-to-.049 engines or with electric motor-powered radio-control models.

Channels

Each of the servo motors in the aircraft is on a separate "channel" so that the motor that moves the rudder, for example, won't accidentally go on when you want to actuate the motor that moves the elevator.

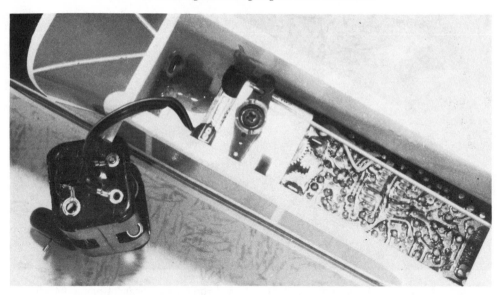

Fig. 5-2   The printed circuit board receiver and a single servo are included in the Cox almost-ready-to-fly "Cub". *Courtesy Cox Hobbies.*

Obviously, the more channels a radio transmitter will control, the more sophisticated the receiver electronics must be and the more expensive the entire unit will be. The servo motors add to the cost of the system as well. You will find some radio transmitters and receivers included in beginner models, like the Cox "Cub", that may have only a single channel. That one channel will usually allow fully proportional control of only the rudder; the engine is set to run at full speed, and the elevator is adjusted or "trimmed" to give the aircraft a level glide. The model will climb gently all the while the engine is running then glide back to earth; the rudder control is needed to keep the model within sight and within range of the radio transmitter. These models are just fine for a beginner or a youngster to learn the basics of flight. For true control, though, the system should have at least two channels so that both the altitude (elevator) and direction (rudder) can be controlled by the flier.

Two channels are enough for most radio-controlled sailplanes and for "trainer" types of powered radio-control aircraft. The powered models are certainly more enjoyable to fly, however, when you have control over the speed of the engine and the ailerons that allow the aircraft to bank into a coordinated turn or to perform rolls. Each of those functions requires an additional channel. Radio-control transmitters and receivers with servo motors are available with three, four, five and more channels. The three-channel setup is probably the biggest "bargain" in that it will provide either aileron control or the engine throttle control a powered aircraft flier wants and the tow hook release and/or the spoiler servo for a sailplane flier. If you insist on more channels, you'll probably be wise to opt for one of the five- or seven-channel rings, because their resale value is much greater than that of the smaller sets. The fifth channel is often controlled by a switch on the top or side of the transmitter, and it may not be fully proportional like the other four channels. The fifth channel is used, on powered aircraft models, to control retractable landing gear, dive brakes, bomb releases, and the like. Expect to spend between $300 and $500 for a five- or seven-channel radio-control transmitter, receiver, and servos.

Frequencies

There are at least 18 different frequencies that have been allocated by the FCC for use by radio-control hobbyists. The frequencies allow up to 18 fliers to fly at the same time without any of them sending a signal from his or her transmitter that might send someone else's model out of control. Each radio and transmitter is furnished with color-coded signal flags which *must* be mounted on the transmitter's antenna so others will know for certain what channel you are using. Most public flying fields and club fields have a "frequency pole" with color-coded clothespins or clips that match all the available radio frequencies. When a flier arrives at the field, he *must* place his frequency pin (the clip that corresponds to his transmitter frequency) on the pole. If someone else comes along later with the

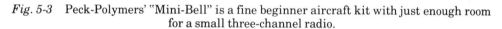

Fig. 5-3   Peck-Polymers' "Mini-Bell" is a fine beginner aircraft kit with just enough room for a small three-channel radio.

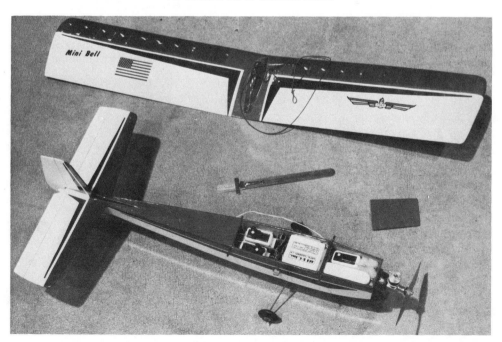

Fig. 5-4 One of the "standard" radio-control setups utilizes the left "stick" on the transmitter to control the left rudder.

Fig. 5-5 Moving the rudder stick to the right should actuate right rudder (shown).

Fig. 5-6 The left control stick usually actuates the elevator. Move the stick up for "down" elevator.

Fig. 5-7 Move the left stick up for "down" elevator. The rudder stick (left) can be operated at the same for a climbing turn.

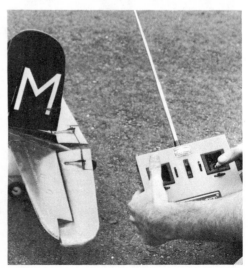

Fig. 5-8 The right and left movements of the *right* transmitter stick usually operate the ailerons on the rear edges of the wings.

Fig. 5-9 Moving the *right* transmitter stick to the left usually activates "up" ailerons (shown), and moving it right activates "down" ailerons.

Fig. 5-10 The up and down movement of the *left* transmitter stick usually actuates the throttle control. The aircraft is a Royal-brand Corsair built by Adam Taylor.

Fig. 5-11   The fifth channel, on many transmitters, is simply a switch on the top or side of
the case. This one actuates the landing flaps.

same frequency, the new arrival can tell at a glance who is already using that frequency. Most experienced fliers buy radio-control sets in the 72-MHz range because there is less interference on those frequencies and several of them are intended solely for model aircraft. Some of the beginner models operate on some special low-power frequencies that don't even require an FFC license.

The radio-control rigs sold for model aircraft use have enough power to control the aircraft for as far as you can see the aircraft. It's wise, though, to check the range of any radio-control rig every time you fly. Simply collapse the antenna (or remove it—check your R/C equipment's owner's manual to see which) and rest the model on the ground. Walk away from it while a friend watches the control surfaces as you operate them with the receiver. Your friend can give you a hand signal to tell you when the control surfaces begin to respond in an erratic and sluggish fashion. Your owner's manual will state how many feet is the normal range for your brand of radio. The power of the radio-control transmitter, the receiver, and the servos is dependent solely on the condition of your batteries. The *only* way to be certain that your batteries are charged is to charge them overnight before *every* flying day. Inexpensive overnight chargers for the ni-cad batteries recommended for radio-control sets are available from most hobby shops. Wise fliers also check their batteries for operation on the flying field with a voltmeter. A quick voltmeter test for battery charge may save the day if a weak cell is discovered.

CHART OF RADIO-CONTROL FREQUENCIES
ASSIGNED TO MODELERS BY THE FCC

AIRCRAFT USE ONLY		AIRCRAFT USE ONLY—NARROW BAND			
Frequency	*Channel No.*	*Frequency*	*Channel No.*	*Frequency*	*Channel No.*
72.550	38	72.030	12	72.270	24
72.550	40	72.070	14	72.310	26
72.630	42	72.110	16	72.350	28
72.670	44	72.150	18	72.390	30
72.710	46	72.190	20	72.430	32
72.750	48	72.230	22	72.470	34
72.790	50				
72.830	52				
72.870	54				
72.910	56				

BOAT/CAR USE ONLY				ALL USES	
Frequency	*Channel No.*	*Frequency*	*Channel No.*	*Frequency*	*Channel No.*
75.430	62	75.750	78	26.995	A1
75.470	64	75.790	80	27.045	A2
75.510	66	75.830	82	27.095	A3
75.550	68	75.870	84	27.145	A4
75.590	70	75.910	86	27.195	A5
75.630	72	75.950	88	27.255	A6
75.670	74	75.990	90		
75.710	76				

On December 20, 1987, it became illegal to operate a radio control transmitter on the following frequencies:
72.080   72.160   72.240   72.320   72.400   72.960   75.640
If you have a transmitter on one of these frequencies, you must send it to your service center to have its frequency changed.
Formerly the frequency 72.030 (Channel 12) was legal for any aircraft use. **On January 1, 1988, this frequency became a narrow band only frequency.** If you have an existing "wide band" radio on this frequency, it will also need to be changed.

Fig. 5-12

Quality Bargains

The chances of your finding a quality radio-control rig at the price of an inexpensive rig are pretty slim unless you're willing to buy a used unit. If you do buy used, do so from a reliable hobby dealer and have an expert go over the equipment before you pay for it. There are several brands of radio *kits* on the market, but their major value lies in whatever pleasure you get from assembling them; they are not appreciably less expensive than already-assembled units. You will eventually need to have your radio and receiver repaired or tuned, so be absolutely certain you buy a brand that has a reputation for availability of both services and parts. You may also want to buy a second "matching" receiver with servo motors so you can fly two different models from the same transmitter (not at the same time, of course). You may need to have the second receiver adjusted or tuned so that it will respond as well as the first receiver to the transmitter's controls.

Be wary of two-channel transmitters with control levers that move in just a single direction. Each lever operates a single channel with this type of setup. These transmitters are common among the "beginner" or inexpensive sets. Their operation is excellent, but you may have difficulty finding a teacher who uses this control mode. The more common radio-control transmitters have two controls on each stick or lever. Moving the lever up and down controls one channel, while moving the lever right or left controls the other. Moving the lever diagonally controls both channels at the same time.

Radio Installation

The radio-control receivers and servo motors are small enough to fit into any kit that has been designed for R/C use. Some of the smaller models, like those with .020 engines, may require the use of the smallest receivers and only two small servos. When you buy the model, check to see if there really is room for whatever receiver and servos you want to use. Fit the receiver and the servo motors as part of the kit-assembly sequence so you can move whatever bulkheads that may be necessary to fit the R/C

Fig. 5-13 A complete four-channel fully-proportional R/C rig with transmitter (center) and (left to right) transmitter aerial, battery pack for the receiver, four servo motors, and receiver. *Courtesy Ace R/C, Inc.*

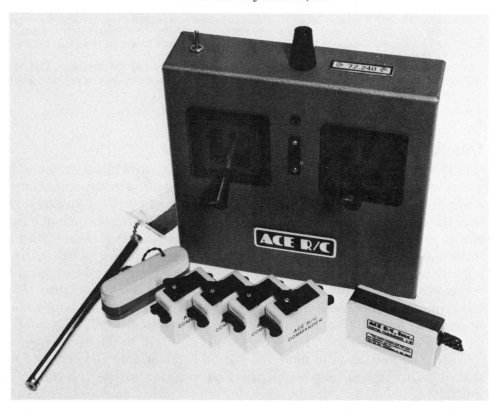

equipment inside the fuselage. This is also the time to install the proper mounting rails ("bearers") and brackets to mount the receiver and servos, while the interior of the fuselage is readily accessible. The radio equipment will alter the model's center of gravity, so you may have to move some of it (especially the batteries) fore or aft. The final assembly stage is the best time for that type of alteration. There's more information in Chapters 2 and 7 on finding the center of gravity.

The radio receiver is a relatively delicate instrument that *must* be protected from motor or engine vibration and landing shocks with some type of foam padding. The batteries must be padded as well. Proper installation (using your owner's manual as a guide) will help to prevent the equipment's tearing loose from the mounts and being damaged needlessly. Use the relatively hard "closed-cell" type foam rubber or use the white plastic type of foam that new radio receivers and transmitters are packed in. The soft foam like that in kitchen sponges allows too much movement and damage may still occur. The softer foam can be used to surround the hard foam as insulation against vibration in models powered with internal combustion engines. The receiver, batteries, and servo should also be sealed inside plastic baggies in powered aircraft models so the fuel cannot reach them.

Servo Motor Mounts

The servo motor must be mounted firmly in the fuselage so its control "commands" are precise. The servo motor can be attached to a piece of hardwood or plywood with bolts or screws, the rubber grommets (furnished with the servos), and the vibration-proof nuts with nylon inserts. The plywood is then epoxied to the fuselage. Just be sure the screws and nuts are accessible (or use epoxy and "blind" nuts). Use LocTite or a similar fluid to keep the screws tight. The servo motor must be positioned so there's an absolutely straight path from the servo wheel or arm to the holes on the control horn on the rudder, elevator, or aileron. You've spent several hundred dollars or more to buy a radio with perfect response, so don't dull that response by using bent control rods between the servo motors and the control horns. Chapter 9 describes some of the best methods for obtaining accurate movement at the hinges of the control surfaces with the control horns and pushrods. Keep the pushrods themselves absolutely straight from the servo wheel's pushrod-mounting hole to the pushrod-mounting hole on the control horn and you'll have the precise control you hope for.

The control of the throttle, landing gear retracts, or any other optional functions need not be as precise as the control of the rudder, ailerons, and elevator. If you do have to position one or more of the servo motors to achieve an offset between the control horn (or the throttle lever) and the servo, do so with the servos that control something other than the

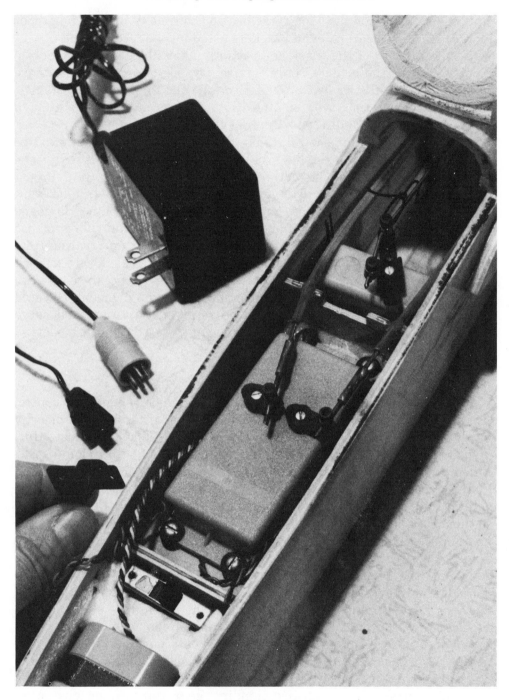

Fig. 5-14 A Kraft-brand "brick" (one-piece receiver and two servos) with a third servo installed in a sailplane. The plugs and sockets connect the ni-cad battery pack to the charger (top).

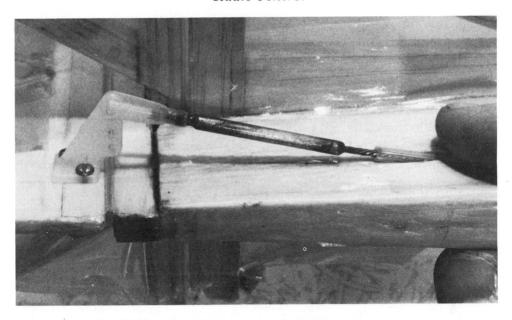

Fig. 5-15   The nylon control horn (left) is attached to the rudder with two screws and nuts. The pushrod is guided out of the fuselage with a short piece of tube. The pushrod pivots on the control horn with a snap-on nylon clevis.

Fig. 5-16   The snap-on clevis links are available to fit the throttle levers on most carburetors and engines. The two knurled screws adjust the carburetor's idle speed and fuel supply (richness).

rudder, ailerons, or elevator. You can even use a length of flexible cable for those "minor" functions (if you must) to keep the "paths" clear for the rudder, aileron, and elevator pushrods to run straight and true. Mount the servos for all of the functions at least an eighth-inch apart so they won't vibrate against each other.

Try the operation of the receiver and servo motors frequently while you assemble the model. Try the action of the elevator, for example, as soon as you have it installed. Try the rudder, too, as soon as it is in place.

TROUBLE-SHOOTING CHART FOR RADIO-CONTROL SYSTEMS

Trouble	Probable Cause	Remedy
Immediately after launch plane veers left or right and does not respond to controls.	Transmitter and/or receiver not "ON".	Be sure transmitter and receiver are "ON".
Rudder does not move or moves erratically.	Transmitter and/or receiver batteries depleted or misaligned. Transmitter or receiver malfunction.	Reposition or replace batteries. If this fails, send transmitter and plane to manufacturer for radio repair.
	Broken wire connections.	Send plane to manufacturer for repair or replacement.
	Control rod from servo to tail is bent.	Bend rod into straight position.
During flight, plane requires constant trim dial adjustment to correct for its tendency to turn left or right	Rudder rod needs adjustment.	Check trim dial on transmitter when plane is down. If the dial has been moved left or right, adjust the rudder rod accordingly, per "Trim Adjustment" section.
Rudder locks to the right.	Interference from other radios in area.	Try flying in a different area.
	Transmitter malfunction.	Send transmitter to manufacturer for repair.
	Transmitter antenna not fully extended.	Fully extend transmitter antenna.
	Your plane has flown out of radio range.	Run after the plane with transmitter held over your head until plane again responds to your controls.

Courtesy of Cox Hobbies.

Fig. 5-17

Remember, you're building a *flying* model aircraft, and those controls must work perfectly. There are standard arrangements for which control stick on the transmitter operates which function on the aircraft. The owner's manual furnished with your R/C set should identify which controls are which. Be certain, for example, that right stick movement on the receiver produces right rudder deflection. When you push the same stick (on the better "gimbal" type of transmitter controls) forward (or upward), the aircraft's elevator should drop down. (We've seen even "experts" arrive at the flying field with a new airplane and watched their embarrassment as they found out that their control response was backwards!) You certainly want to learn to fly with "standard" control response and, once you do learn, you certainly don't want to have to start all over again just because you didn't spend the time to get the servos installed properly.

Fig. 5-18 The new Cox ready-to-fly R/C "E/Z Bee" has foam construction with a built-in single channel radio. *Courtesy Cox Hobbies.*

Chapter 6
✈
Flight Magic

Radio control is the fulfillment of the dreams of generations of model aircraft fliers—one of those rare instances where a science-fiction kind of fantasy comes to life. Radio control has the potential of allowing you to control a model aircraft just as though you were sitting in the cockpit. We must warn you that radio control has only the *potential* for the fulfillment of that dream of remote control flight; you still need the practice to control the aircraft properly, and you need the right type of radio-control equipment with a model that also has the potential of allowing you to fly the way you wish. We've described the basics of aerodynamics and the radio-control systems in earlier chapters. This is the one where all that theory goes together in actual flight.

The No-Crash System

There are some "secrets" to flying a radio-control aircraft that many of the instruction manuals and many instructors take for granted. You can avoid most crashes if you remember two fundamentals: (1) keep the aircraft's *air speed* up *at all times,* and (2) understand that almost any aircraft will automatically bank when in a turn and, when it does, the elevator now will be used to adjust the radius of the turn—"neutral" rudder should, then, return the plane to normal flight. We're getting way ahead of ourselves in any basic flight lesson sequence, but these "secrets" apply to virtually every maneuver the aircraft will make. Memorize these two so thoroughly that your subconscious will feed them into your mind *before* telling your fingers to make *any* control change during flight. If you can do that, you'll avoid about 90 percent of the crashes that most newcomers make.

Flying by radio control is a totally new experience, even for one who is already an accomplished pilot of full-size aircraft. You will have very few "learned" responses to bring into the sport to help you. In other words, everyone has to *learn* to fly by radio control. This is like any other learning experience that requires the use of your own body's "motor" reflexes; it takes carefully controlled first lessons and perfect repetitions to get everything right, so do whatever you can to get an already accomplished radio-control model aircraft flier to teach you personally.

76

Fig. 6-1   The transmitter aerial is pointed in the direction of flight to help this flier to visualize the working of the aircraft's controls.

Most experienced fliers will be more than happy to stand by during that learning flight. You may find help through the hobby shop where you bought your aircraft and radio (one reason—the other is repair service—why we cannot recommend that you buy by mail or from a discount store). You may want to join a local flying club where some of the members will be willing to teach you. Some shops and clubs even have "buddy box" radio transmitter setups that function a lot like the driver training automobiles with two steering wheels and other controls. The control transmitter in the instructor's hands is connected to "your" transmitter in such a way that the instructor can correct any mistakes you make or may merely control, say, the elevator while you concentrate on learning to master the rudder. The disadvantage of the system is that you really don't learn to fly with your own transmitter. If you do learn with the "buddy box" system, try to buy a transmitter with control almost identical to the one you learned with so you'll have a similar "feeling" at the controls when you fly "solo". You can probably learn to fly sooner, regardless of who teaches you, if you remember *always* to hold the transmitter so that the antenna points in the direction the plane is going. If you follow it around in this fashion, there is less chance of becoming disoriented during those times when the aircraft is flying toward you or above you. This also eliminates the problem of trying to reverse the rudder control when the aircraft flies towards you.

Your instructor will know immediately why your aircraft is not flying in the direction you "think" it should when you first try to operate the transmitter control sticks. The instructor can, then, tell you immediately how to correct the controls so you skip most of the frustrating trial-and-error type of learning. That expert help is only a shortcut, however, because the real learning takes place only by doing and doing and doing and doing. Your learning will be much faster if you can manage to put two or more flying sessions back to back. Try to arrange for both a Saturday and a Sunday morning so your *body*'s motor functions will still remember how to respond to the visual inputs—"fly again before you forget the details" is another way of stating the same thing. Better yet, try to fit three or four early evening flights together. Once you have truly learned to fly, you can go away from it for years and still retain much of the ability. It's that first learning that is so easy to forget. This is one of the most demanding hand-to-eye coordination sports there is.

Finally, check the range of the radio and "pre-flight" check the aircraft before *every* flight to be absolutely certain that all of the rubber bands for the wings are new, that all the radio connections are tight, that the batteries have a fresh overnight charge, that every control functions properly and instantly to actual radio commands from the transmitter, and that the aircraft and radio are working perfectly. If this is your first flight with a new airplane, a new radio, or any single new component in either "system", test-glide the model to be sure that its center of gravity is still in the right place. Launch it into the wind with enough force for it to glide level for about 75 feet. If the model is powered with an engine larger than about .10 cubic inch, you'll have to have the engine on for that test flight with just enough fuel for a short engine run.

Your First Radio-Control Aircraft

The aircraft you use for those first flights is a very important element in the learning process; the larger and more complex models are actually more difficult to fly than the trainers. You most certainly will crash many times while you are learning so get your ego prepared for it. When you accept that fact, you should be a bit more willing to settle for an aircraft with just two-channel control. You can still purchase one of the better five- or more-channel radio rigs if you wish and use only two of the channels. If you want to learn to fly a powered model, something like a Cox "S-Tee" or "Q-Tee" or a Sig "Kadet", an MRC "Trainer Hawk", or a Carl Goldberg "Ranger", each with the engine that the kit manufacturer recommends, is a good place to start. The sailplanes with electric power, like Cox's "Sportavia" or Astro Flight's kits, are also excellent training

Fig. 6-2 The inexpensive single-channel R/C almost-ready-to-fly models, like this Cox "Cub," are excellent aircraft for beginners. Cox has recently introduced a new R/C "E-Z Bee" model to supersede the "Cub." *Courtesy Cox Hobbies.*

aircraft for two-channel control. If you are going to learn radio-control soaring, pick a model with about a 72-inch wingspan rather than one of the larger sailplanes. The two channels should be connected so they control the rudder and elevator; the engines in the powered models can remain on full-throttle for the learning flights to allow you to concentrate on those two most fundamental controls.

Many of you will make your first flight with a model that has a single channel. This is the least expensive type of radio-control model, and you can learn a great deal about radio-control flying with one. The single channel will normally control the rudder. The elevator should be adjusted before each flight to provide a shallow glide. If your first flight is with a sailplane, a rubber band launching system like a "Hi-Start" will provide the energy to get the model in the air. Once there, it will be up to you to try to steer the model into thermals and over the edges of slopes to catch upward wind currents for a sustained flight. If you find yourself caught in a wind or headed straight for some obstacle, you can use the rudder to help turn quickly. Another secret of radio-control flying is that the model will turn an ever-tighter circle as long as you keep the rudder turned to its full angle. Eventually, that turn will become so tight that the model will go into a spiral dive if you aren't quick enough to "catch" it by applying neutral (straight-ahead) or opposite rudder. It takes a whole lot of nerve to turn the nose of the plane straight down when that is exactly what you are trying to avoid, but that's the first step in spin recovery! Next, apply a small amount of rudder in the direction opposite the spin and, as soon as the model begins to turn, return to neutral rudder, and the model should resume level flight. This advice makes up a sort of advanced flying lesson, even for a model with two or more channels, but these "secrets" are something that you must add to your "no-crash" mind conditioning if you are flying with just one channel. Those with two-channel control can use the same technique to get their aircraft into a spin (either accidentally or on purpose), but they have control over two axes and are better equipped to recover from a dive or a spin.

The First Flight

Find a flying field that is mostly grass or soft weeds with 100 feet or so of smooth and level dirt (if you are flying a model with landing wheels or an engine-powered model). You'll minimize the chances of serious landing damage by letting the weeds cushion the first few landings. When you become proficient at landings, you can use the dirt as a landing strip. Save those landings on concrete or blacktop for your fifth or sixth lesson. Always be sure to launch and to land into the wind so your ground speed will be less; this will make the aircraft more controllable. Most crashes occur at landing or takeoff because the aircraft goes through a stage when it is flying too slow for the wings to provide "lift", and it noses down into a diving crash. A small amount of wind (about five miles per hour or less) will help to avoid a stall; don't attempt to fly on days when the wind is blowing any faster than that.

Throw the model into the wind with the nose slightly down, using the same technique you learned to check its center of gravity. This time, though, be sure to have the engine or motor on and running perfectly. If the elevator controls were adjusted properly during the test glide, the spring control on the transmitter lever will automatically keep the elevator (and rudder) in a neutral or level flight and straight ahead as well. Apply just a slight amount of "up" elevator control as soon as you can, with both hands back on the transmitter. Let the model climb at about a 15-to-20-degree angle until it reaches about a 200-to-300-foot altitude. You may have to alternate a bit between almost "neutral" and slightly "up" elevator to keep the climb steady. You will also have to apply a bit of right or left rudder control to keep the model from going out of sight. Try to keep the model crossing back and forth in front of you so it appears to climb in a sawtooth pattern; this will minimize the amount of time the model is flying directly toward you, and you won't become disoriented as to which is right or left.

Fig. 6-3   The Cox "Sportavia" is available with either a fuel-burning engine or an electric motor. It's designed for two-channel R/C. *Courtesy Cox Hobbies.*

Fig. 6-4 You can launch an R/C sailplane by hand if there's a fairly stiff breeze and some hope of finding thermals. This is a Midwest "Hawk."

The turns are the tricky part of any flight. When you apply rudder, the nose of the model will probably drop a little and, if the turn is too tight, the model will continue to dive, so be ready for a little "up" elevator control. If you apply too much "up" elevator, in the middle of a banked turn, the elevator will act like the rudder to pull the aircraft into an even tighter turn. Be content with losing just a bit of altitude on the turns. You can minimize the loss of altitude and the danger of a spiral dive by keeping the turns very broad—enough so that your upward flight is a continued series of ess turns (when viewed from directly below the aircraft). It will appear to be a sawtooth pattern if you keep the model at about a 45-degree angle to your line of sight; direct overhead flights can also be disorienting at first, so keep the model well in front of you. When the model reaches that 200-to-300-foot altitude, simply return to "neutral" elevator and continue either a series of those esses or set the rudder for a slight right or left turn and let the aircraft circle until it runs out of fuel. If you are flying a sailplane launched with a "Hi-Start", it will get the aircraft up to altitude, and you'll use the ess turns and large circles to glide it back down.

Happy Landings

The trip back to the ground can be particularly difficult with a powered model aircraft. For that first flight or so you would be wise to fly the model back down under power until it reaches an altitude of about 100 feet. Hold that altitude until the engine runs out of fuel. The secret of landings is to keep the airspeed up by letting the model descend at its own rate of speed by holding "neutral" or slightly "down" elevator. The aircraft must be landed into the wind, so maneuver it into a position upwind of you when it still has 40 to 50 feet of altitude. By now, you know how quickly it will loose altitude for any given amount of distance. The flight with the wind is called the "downwind leg" of the flight pattern. The illustration (Fig. 6-6) shows a straight path across the wind for the "base leg" of the landing pattern, but a large circle (Fig. 6-7) is a better bet for those first few landings. Any sharp application of rudder will most certainly send the model into a shallow dive at these low landing speeds, so barely touch that rudder lever. Do not try for a pinpoint landing; land over a 100 yards of grass, if you can, so you can let the aircraft decide when it's ready to touch down. When the aircraft is a foot or so above the ground, apply just a trace of "up" elevator control to level the aircraft for a wheels-first (rather than propeller-first) landing. If you apply too much "up" elevator, the model will stall. If the nose does come up, return instantly to "neutral" elevator

Fig. 6-5 Have the transmitter ready, at the moment of launch, so you can manipulate the controls for maximum lift.

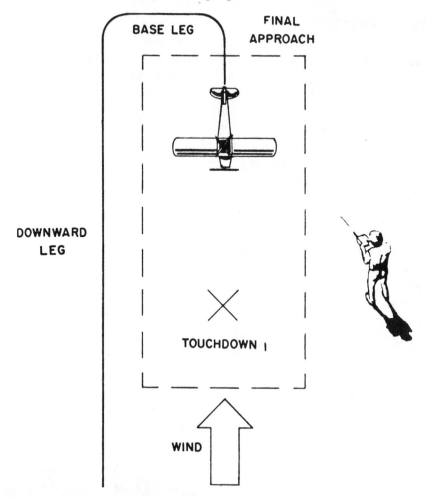

Fig. 6-6 The "perfect" landing pattern begins with just enough elevation on the downwind leg for perfect touchdown on the final approach. *Courtesy Cox Hobbies.*

(or even a touch of "down" elevator), then let the aircraft postpone its landing point. Do not alter the positions of the controls until the aircraft has rolled or skidded to a complete stop. Pick up the model and go through a complete inspection and control operation check immediately.

Advanced Flying Techniques

We hope we've instilled a healthy respect in your reflexes for the aircraft's response to rudder and stabilizer. As you gain flying confidence, you'll begin to try maneuvers that can have a disastrous effect on that other all-important "no-crash" tip: keep the airspeed up. Gusts of wind and wind changes at 200 feet and more can affect the aircraft's airspeed considerably without any noticeable change in its ground speed. Remember, it's the speed of the wind over the wings and control surfaces

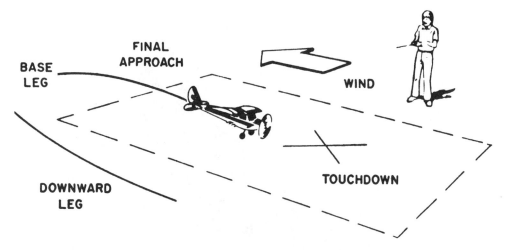

Fig. 6-7   A side view of the same "perfect" landing pattern shown in Figure 6-6. *Courtesy Cox Hobbies.*

Fig. 6-8   They say "Any landing is a *good* landing!" This Byron Originals' ⅓ scale "Pitts" R/C model was landing with the nose too far up to suit the flier.

Fig. 6-9 The flier over-corrected and landed nose first. He made it without nosing over or breaking the propeller!

that makes the aircraft fly. If the wind is from the tail of the aircraft, the aircraft may appear to have plenty of airspeed when, in fact, it is almost ready to stall and fall into a dive. You'll notice a very sluggish response to the controls when the airspeed decreases. You can run into trouble with airspeed when the aircraft is climbing, too. If you apply too much "up" elevator, you'll bring the aircraft too close to its stall speed. Again, you'll begin to feel a sluggish response from the controls when the aircraft comes close to its stall speed.

There's no problem orienting yourself to the model's control surfaces when it is flying away from you and only a small degree of disorientation when it's flying right or left across your field of vision. When it's flying toward you, however, the right and left controls for the rudder and (if it's a three-or-more-channel 'craft) the aileron controls will operate "backwards". This can be dangerous when the aircraft is in a banked position, because you may very well apply the opposite correction for a dive. Most fliers use the simple trick of pushing the lever in the control lever *toward* the direction the aircraft is already going. Practice flying towards yourself until you can manipulate the controls as well that way as with the model flying away from you. If you have trouble, try imagining yourself in the cockpit of the model rather than on the ground. Perfect *both* right and left turns (most of us find one or the other a whole lot easier) and directly overhead flights.

Aileron Rolls

If you are flying a model that has a third channel for aileron control, you'll be able to use the ailerons to help control the degree of bank in a turn. The aileron control is a third control to "balance" between the rudder and elevator for the amount of bank and nicely coordinated turns you wish, so you must have those first two working perfectly together first. The ailerons can, of course, be used to perform gentle roll manuevers. If the roll is too sudden, you may unexpectedly find yourself inverted. A bit of "up" elevator, eased in and out during the inverted phase of the roll, will keep the nose up and the aircraft level and help keep the maneuver crisp and controllable. You can combine half a loop (for a "C"-shape maneuver) and half a roll to duplicate the "Immelmann turn" that the pilots of full-size aerobatic aircraft love so much. The Immelmann turn begins and ends with the aircraft flying at a level altitude; the roll is accomplished at the same time, so the aircraft is halfway through the roll during the vertical phase of the half-loop.

Fig. 6-10 Bill Love is walking his "pattern" or aerobatic R/C biplane down the runway before takeoff with the transmitter aerial pointed toward the aircraft's flight path.

Pattern Flying

The basic aerobatic or pattern maneuver is a simple "inside loop" where the aircraft does a 360-degree loop beginning with "up" elevator control. The basic inside and outside loop patterns and wingovers are illustrated in chapter 4. If you try a loop with a sailplane, be sure you have at least 100 feet of altitude, and begin the maneuver with a bit of "down" elevator to build up airspeed. Try about half of the elevator control at first, but be ready to use less if the aircraft's flying speed slows too much during the vertical and inverted portions of the maneuver. The worst that is likely to happen is a stall, and you should know how to correct that by now. The chances of such a stall will be less if you are sure to enter the maneuver with the rudder absolutely neutral and flying with the wind so the wind can give you some extra lift from the vertical to inverted portion of the loop. With practice, you can take advantage of the increased airspeed at the end of the loop to begin a second or third consecutive loop. You'll likely lose a bit of altitude with each loop, so keep your peripheral vision alert.

Outside loops will be extremely difficult to perform with most aircraft that have dihedral in the wings and with aircraft that have flat-bottomed airfoil wing cross sections. A model with symmetrically shaped airfoils, little dihedral, and aileron control is the one to use for true radio-control pattern flying. Obviously, you'll need plenty of altitude for an outside loop and plenty of airspeed. You can go on to figure eight maneuvers once you've mastered the inside and outside loops. If your model doesn't really want to perform those outside loops, you can still do figure eights (if you have aileron control) by combining a series of four Immelmann turns; an alternate right and left for a figure ess, then an "outside" pair of Immelmann turns for another ess to complete the figure eight. All of this will be far easier with one of the "pattern" or stunt R/C aircraft with a .40-to-.60 engine. The AMA has several competition categories for radio-control pattern aircraft, and it's one of those rather rare competition categories where the aircraft last so long they literally wear out.

Thermal Soaring

The radio-control sailplanes, both with and without power, are most enjoyable to fly in the virtually invisible updrafts of hot air called "thermals". The thermal is simply a bubble of hot air that is formed over a dark-colored field or parking lot or building top by the sun. The bubble rises above the ground or building top in such a way that the effect is one of what appear to be "gusts" of ascending wind currents. When you see a falcon or hawk circling in the sky, the chances are he is riding a thermal to gain altitude. The sailplane modelers in your area will be able to direct you to the flying sites where thermals are common. With experience, you'll be able to find some of your own. A model sailplane can rise as high

Fig. 6-11   With practice, you'll be able to touchdown right on the landing ribbon during R/C sailplane competition flying.

as 5000 feet in minutes on a thermal; flights of 1000 feet or more are common.

The best way to try to "catch" a thermal is to set the model into a very gentle banked turn about 100-to-200 feet in diameter over a suspected thermal area. Watch the model as it circles and see if there isn't one area of the sky where it suddenly gains altitude. When you find that area, try to fly across it to find its boundaries and then turn back in and establish another circle that will keep the aircraft well within the boundaries of the thermal. A thermal is not necessarily round, but the large-diameter circle is the easiest way to stay within it without constant changes in control. The thermal may drift slightly with the wind, but so will your sailplane, so it's not all that difficult to stay inside the thermal once you've learned how to find it.

Chapter 7

Free Flight

If you want to discover the true magic of flight, the model aircraft that fall into the category of "free flight" are the ones that have the keys to that kingdom. The history of the hobby is based on free-flight models; dozens of the kits that were introduced before World War II are still on the market. When anything lasts that long, it must have something to offer. Free flight is the model aircraft category for the builder who wants to display his or her skills at the almost ancient craft of assembling balsa wood sticks and covering them with tissue, silk, or (today) sheet plastic. The Don Quixotes of modeling who love to fight odds are the most avid free-flight modelers, for free flight is a challenge. The modern kits feature mostly die-cut parts, but the models are still assembled with an airframe that is built from the inside out just about like a full-size aircraft. If the assembly is perfect, so everything is in perfect alignment with absolute minimal weight (grams and tenths of an ounce count, here), then there's a good chance the model will fly well.

Classes

The hobby of flying model aircraft began with free flight, so you can guess that there are a whole lot of different ways that those hobby pioneers found to fly their models. Each of those different methods of flying without the benefit of either control lines or radios resulted in a different class of free-flight competition and in different ·types of free-flight kits and plans. The most popular class of free-flight aircraft will do something that's not practical with the other types of aircraft models—they'll fly indoors. Indoor classes for AMA competition include Peanut Scale for those "stick model" replicas of propeller-driven aircraft with wingspan less than 13 inches. The propellers on the models are driven by twisted rubber bands. The kits made by Peck Polymers, Flyline, Micro-X and Sterling are the most popular with competitors. The most readily available stick models are those made by firms like Cleveland, Comet, Guillow, Sterling, and Top-Flite, but most of these have a wingspan large enough to put them in the AMA "Indoor Rubber Flying Scale" class for models with wingspans of less than 30 inches. Many of these rubber-powered models can be equipped with internal combustion engines and radio receivers or control lines, but that puts them in something other

Fig. 7-1 Peck-Polymers' "One Night 28" is designed to fly perfectly, regardless of appearance. *Courtesy Peck-Polymers.*

than the rubber-powered category. Any of these "indoor" models can, of course, be flown outdoors on a calm day. By now you might expect to discover that there are also "non-scale" models that will generally fly better than any of these scale kits in the hands of most of us. There are, of course, AMA competition classes for those "rubber-powered" models that include both indoor and outdoor competition. These classes include models like the microfilm-covered models (Fig. 7-13) and the gliders made from sheet balsa wood.

Most outdoor competition is centered around models that do not resemble any type of full-size aircraft. The most popular free-flight models for outdoor flying are those powered by the same type of engines as the control-line models. The .049 or ¹⁄₂A engines are the most common, but there are competition categories and kits for models using engines with as much as .60-cubic-inch displacement. There is even a free-flight class for powered helicopters, if you really think you're an expert. The outdoor categories include both rubber-powered and non-powered models as well, with some highly sophisticated rules. The flying model rockets described in *The ETV Model Book,* also published by Chilton, would fall into the free-flight category, too.

Peanut and Jumbo Scale

These scale "stick models" are a fine diversion for a control-line or radio-control modeler who wants to learn something about miniature building techniques and the tuning (more properly called "trim") adjustments needed for a perfect flight. Perfect stability and flight are basic to a

Fig. 7-2   Hildie Boehme is assembling a
free-flight kit: Peck Polymers' "ROG."

free-flight model because, once the model is in the air, the flier has
absolutely no control over it. You might call any free-flight model a type
of "trained bird", in that it can be assembled and adjusted to fly in a
certain pattern. A typical powered free-flight model is "programmed" to
fly upward in a steady spiral until it runs out of power; it is then supposed
to descend to the ground in a circular pattern. It's a lot more difficult than
it sounds, because the model must be trimmed to compensate for the
torque and power of its rubber band or fuel-burning engine *and* for a
gliding flight—and either one of those is difficult enough by itself;
remember, even a single-channel radio-control aircraft has a movable
rudder to compensate for powered versus non-powered flight. Adjusting
the center of gravity, motor angle, stabilizer, and rudder for a "perfect"
upward powered free-flight and a perfect glide is one of the most
challenging aspects of the hobby.

Weight is the number one enemy of any free-flight model. The experts
go so far as to substitute smaller sticks for those supplied in the kits. Don't
try that, though, until you've assembled at least three or four stock kits
and made them fly properly. Your first model should be one with a fairly
large stabilizer and plenty of dihedral in the wings; very few low-winged
models have both those features, so you'd be happier with the flight
characteristics of a high-wing model. Absolute precision is the key to
building any free-flight model, so take your time to be sure that everything is square and that there are no warps in the wings, rudder, or
stabilizer. Most modelers don't add the weight and possible warp that a
painted paper surface can give; they fly their models with the tissue

covering unpainted. Repairs are much easier with an unpainted model, too. The paper covering can be stretched to build in a slight amount of warp in the left wing so that the tip of the wing angles a slight bit more upward at its forward edge than at the rear. This is called "wash-in", and it will enable the model to hold a circular glide pattern with more stability than achievable by using only the rudder. The effect is similar to having a "down" aileron on the left wing. It can also help a bit to counteract the model's reaction to the torque of the spinning propeller.

Indoor Flight

You might be surprised to learn that the flying conditions inside a gymnasium can vary considerably from one part of the room to the other. There are almost always updrafts in some part of the room that result

Fig. 7-3   Mike Janos launches his Flyline Models' Heinkel 100D rubber-powered free-flight model on a successful flight.

Fig. 7-4 George Batiuk demonstrates the launching technique he finds successful for indoor free-flight models.

from open doors, ventilators in the ceiling, or air conditioning or heater ducts. Your indoor flying model must be trimmed so it will fly in circles that are about equal to one-half to two-thirds the width of the narrowest portion of the indoor flying area. This will give you enough room to maneuver your launching site in the room to take advantage of the most consistent air. The chart (Fig. 2-10) in Chapter 2 will give you the corrections needed to get the model flying absolutely straight. Those adjustments will also allow you to adjust the angle of the propeller *shaft* for a slight upward climb while trimming the model itself for a power-off slight downward glide. The only "fiddling" adjustment you'll then have to make is to trim the stabilizer or "wash in" the wing to compensate for the torque of the motor. Be sure to note that the motor torque can give the model a small degree of bank when the power is on. When you test-glide the model to determine how it flies, try it both with and without the motor. You'll have to add enough rudder angle so the model will fly in a circle with the power on, or it will simply fly into a wall.

Most rules allow you to choose between a hand-launch and an "ROG" (rise-off-ground) takeoff, but you'll have at least four more feet of possible elevation if you can perfect your ROG takeoffs. Contests (and just plain fascinating flights) are centered around the duration of the flight. It's difficult to hand-launch a model at the proper angle and speed for the propeller to do its work immediately. Most fliers lose as much of their rubber power during those first moments of hand-launch glide as they

Fig. 7-5 Indoor free-flight scale models are often fascinating little machines like this Peck-Polymers "Baby Ace". *Courtesy Peck-Polymers.*

would by allowing the model to pull itself along the ground for its own takeoff. Give the model the slightest little shove, as you release the propeller, to help it overcome the inertia and to get it pointed straight ahead for take-off.

Trim Tabs

Trim tabs are simply small pieces of paper or aluminum or plastic sheet stock that are glued to the rear surfaces of the rudder, elevator, or wings to make delicate adjustments in the aircraft's flying stability. Trim tabs are the smaller, secondary flaps on full-size aircraft. For the optimum indoor flight, adjust the model to fly in a left circle so the motor torque will help bank the model for a tight climbing circle. The circle will become larger as the motor torque and energy is expended. You can adjust the diameter of that circle by as little as six inches by simply adding a ⅛-x-½-inch trim tab to the rear of the rudder and bending the tab in or out. Trim tabs should not be required on the wings, because you can get the same effect with a little "wash-in". You may, however, want to add trim tabs to the model right at the flying site to compensate for unusual updrafts or a high degree of humidity.

Rubber Power

Rubber bands are the source of power for indoor models, and they're also used on some classes of outdoor free flight. If your local dealer doesn't have it, you can order special rubber from the firms that specialize in indoor scale-model kits. These same firm also sell special propellers in a

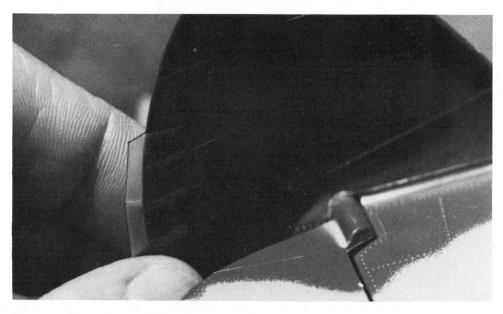

Fig. 7-6   Trim tabs are seldom shown on kit plans. Most are just pieces of business card or thin plastic taped or glued in place.

Fig. 7-7   Many of the powered free-flight kits, like this Cox "Q-Tee" kit, can be used for R/C flying as well. The wings are held by rubber bands to rip free in the event of a crash. *Courtesy Cox Hobbies.*

variety of diameters and pitch angles. Buy an assortment of propellers, extra rubber, and rubber lubricant for your model and one of the commercial hand-crank units to wind the rubber bands. The rubber bands can be about half again the length of the fuselage. The commercial winder will allow you to count the number of turns so you can put in as many as the rubber will stand without breaking. Test fly with only about 100 turns. Stretch the rubber band as you begin to crank it tight. When you've wound in about half the total number of turns, start walking toward the aircraft to allow the rubber to retract as you wind it. You'll break a lot of rubber bands and maybe even tear out a rear "engine" mount or two learning how tight you can wind it. The rubber lubricant (use castor oil if you cannot find special model lubricant) will help, but the only way to learn is to try it for yourself.

Outdoor Free Flight

If you really want to combine sport with the hobby of flying model aircraft, pick outdoor free flight. Most outdoor free-flight flying fields that clubs use are at least a mile square. The clubs generally have a small trailbike to use in chasing down the models, but a lot of people do it on foot. You can easily run ten miles in an afternoon of free-flight flying. You

Fig. 7-8 The design used for Sig's "ABC Scrambler" kit has won several AMA national contests in powered free-flight classes. *Courtesy Sig Manufacturing Co., Inc.*

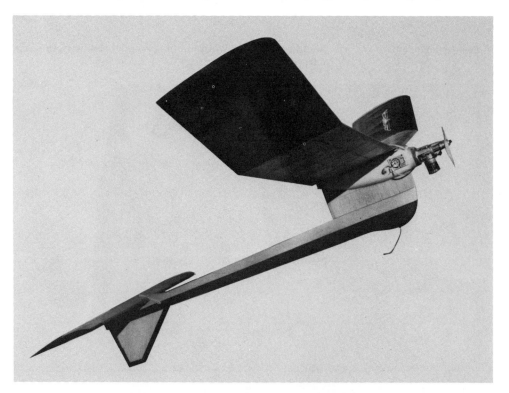

Fig. 7-9   George Batiuk designed and built this AMA class A-2 towline free-flight glider. Note the wing construction to avoid warps.

Fig. 7-10   The entire vertical stabilizer pivots upward under spring tension with this type of free-flight "dethermalizer."

Fig. 7-11   A wind-up mechanism is used for this timer (left). The timer releases the dethermalizer after a pre-set number of minutes.

Fig. 7-12   The propeller blades fold back against the fuselage *after* the rubber power is exhausted on Edward Collins' Wakefield-class aircraft. He built the model to a design by Jim Taylor.

Fig. 7-13   Indoor rubber-powered "endurance" free-flight models like this one weigh just a few grams and can fly for 15 to 20 minutes.

can control the flight of a radio-control aircraft so it will not be diverted away from the launching site by winds. A free-flight model can be controlled only by adjusting the "dethermalizing" device *before* takeoff to limit the time of the gliding portion of the flight. You can, of course, control the duration of the flight by limiting the length of the towline for gliders or by using less fuel in an engine-powered free-flight model. The rubber-powered models seldom reach altitudes where wind drift is much of a problem except with competition class models like the Wakefield-class models.

The visual differences between a powered free-flight model and a similar radio-control aircraft are very subtle, but they are there. There is also a difference in the design of a free-flight glider as compared to a radio-control sailplane. For now, all you need to know is that they are different; so you'll select a free flight kit or plan, if that's really what you want. Most free-flight models are designed so that the stabilizer can flip up into a vertical position at the end of the flight. This is called a "dethermalizer" because it destroys the lift of the aircraft. It's the only way that a free-flight model can be guaranteed to come back to earth. Free-flight models have been known to stay aloft for hours and to drift for ten miles when a dethermalizer failed to function. The stabilizer is simply hinged at the forward end with a rubber band or piano wire spring to tilt it firmly up into a vertical position. A small hook holds the rear of the dethermalizer (stabilizer) down during the flying portion of the flight. The hook is released by a burning piece of rope fuse sold especially for this purpose or by a wind-up clockwork-style timer and release cable. When the dethermalizer pops up, the aircraft will go into a gentle diving spin toward the ground. R/M Enterprises, Sig, Charles Werle, and Doug Galbraith are a few of the specialist firms that have kits and supplies for the free-flight modeler. Their catalogs often provide hints and ideas that can make this aspect of the hobby/sport even more fun.

Chapter 8
Helicopters

The helicopter is one of the technological "breakthroughs" of our time. The concept of hovering flight is almost as old as man's dream of winged flight, and experiments with "autogyros" and other rotating-wing aircraft are about as old as the century. The helicopter itself became practical only after World War II. Model-aircraft enthusiasts have been trying to get model helicopters to fly for almost as long. There are several toy-like helicopters that fly with a spring-wound motor, and Cox even makes one with a fuel-burning engine. These models are strictly free flight, and the only "control" available is the whim of the winds that move them. True hovering flight is a far more complex proposition. Several manufacturers have solved the problem, however, and they offer kits that an experienced modeler can assemble without any machine work. American R/C Helicopters, Inc., Rotary Wing Concepts, Miniature Aircraft USA, Larry Jolley Concepts, and Schluter all offer scale-model helicopters in North America, and there are about a half-dozen other brands available in Japan and Europe.

Hovering Flight

The fundamental principle of a helicopter is that it *does not want to fly.* A stable aircraft will glide to the ground or be carried aloft by simple updrafts or thermals. That just doesn't work with a helicopter, because one of the basics of the design is that it generates its own lift with those gigantic rotor blades. Those blades supply their own energy for the "lift" that a wing has, as we discussed in the second chapter. It's man's only way of "flapping" wings for flight; these "wings," (the rotor blades) however, are spun through the air sideways rather than moved up and down and flexed. The same basic principles of "lift" and "angle of attack" that apply to a fixed-wing aircraft apply to a helicopter. If you expect to understand how a helicopter flies or how to fly one, you first have to understand the basics of fixed-wing aircraft flight.

The term "fixed-wing" is usually applied only to a conventional aircraft when it is being compared to a helicopter. The term is an excellent one, because it gives a fundamental description (by inference, at least) of what a helicopter really is: an aircraft with moving wings. The controls that affect the rotors must, then, have the same effect that the controls of

Fig. 8-1   John Gorham has complete control over his Schluter "Heli-Boy" R/C "beginner" helicopter.

a fixed-wing aircraft do to change the amount of "lift" available. There are two ways to increase or decrease the "lift" that a helicopter has: (1) increase the speed of the rotor rotation (similar to increasing the airspeed of a fixed-wing airplane) and (2) change the pitch of the rotors by pivoting them (similar to changing the "angle of attack" of a fixed-wing aircraft). That's just how a helicopter gains or loses altitude. With a careful and delicate adjustment of the rotor speed and/or the rotor pitch, the helicopter can be made to do magic; it can be made to remain suspended almost motionless in midair in what is known as "hovering flight".

Fig. 8-2   The Cox free-flight "Sky-Copter" has an .020-cubic-inch engine and a built-in "autorotation" feature. *Courtesy Cox Hobbies.*

Forward Flight

A helicopter can be made to fly forward simply by the proper control of its rotors. It appears that that small propeller on the rear of the helicopter would be used to send it forward, but that's *not* what it's for. The small rear propeller is called a "tail rotor", and its primary function is to counteract the torque reaction from the main rotor so the helicopter won't go spinning around instead of the rotor. Most tail rotors are geared to the same shaft as the main rotors so they spin at the same speed as the main rotor. On sophisticated models, the pitch of the tail rotor blades may even be adjustable to compensate for changes in the torque of the main rotor and the effect it may have on the aircraft's stability. It takes a rather drastic change in the pitch of the main rotors to make the helicopter begin to spin about in the air on the axis of the main rotor shaft. For most model flying, it's enough to be able to bring the model back to earth for a manual or screw thread adjustment of the tail rotor's pitch. That pitch adjustment can be used, too, to point the nose of the helicopter in the proper direction so it does have some value. It is generally what is controlled by a fifth channel on the more sophisticated helicopter models.

Some of the modern helicopters have a jet engine mounted between the rotor and the top of the fuselage that is used to give them forward speeds in the 100-plus-miles-per-hour range. So far, that feature appears only on a few experimental scale-model helicopters. It is certainly *not* the usual means by which a helicopter gains forward speed. The rotors on both radio-control model and full-size helicopters are mounted on a pivoting plate called a "swash plate". This plate is generally free to pivot about 5 degrees in any direction so that the complete rotor unit including the rotor's vertical shaft is tilted. There's a universal joint in the rotor shaft to allow this. When the swash plate is tilted forward even one degree, the rotors begin to act as rotors *and* as propeller blades. Part of the "lift" is directed to the front to give the helicopter forward motion. The swash plate can also be tilted to either side to give the helicopter right or left motion or ground speed. The swash plate can be tilted to the rear if the helicopter flier wants to "back up" in the air.

Radio-Control Helicopters

Most of the radio-control helicopters are controlled by four-channel radio transmitters and receivers exactly like those used for fixed-wing models. You can, in fact, in a helicopter use the same radio you use for an airplane by purchasing an additional receiver and four servo motors. Two of the channels will control the right-and-left and fore-and-aft tilt of the swash plate to give the model directional control. The third channel will control the throttle on the helicopter's engine to increase or decrease the speed of the main rotor (and, through the geared shaft, the tail rotor). The fourth channel controls the variable pitch (usually called "collective pitch" in catalogs and ads) of the main rotors. Some of the "trainer" helicopters have rotors with fixed pitch, but the "aerobatic" models all

Fig. 8-3 The Kavan "Bell Jet Ranger" R/C helicopter is available with a number of optional features, including "Collective pitch" rotors.

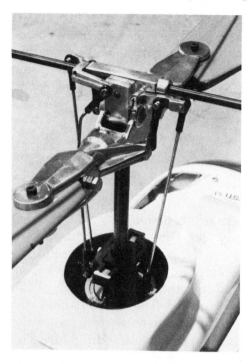

Fig. 8-4   The pushrods leading down to the body of this Kavan helicopter model maintain the rotor pitch even when the "swash plate" is tilted.

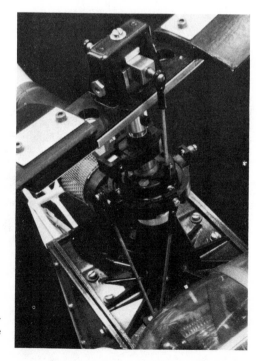

Fig. 8-5   The rotor blade pitch can be adjusted by radio control on this "collective pitch" rotor head by Kavan.

Fig. 8-6 The four-bladed rotor system used on many of the Schluter R/C helicopter kits. *Courtesy Gorham Associates.*

have movable rotor pitch that is controlled with ball-ended pushrods very much like those that control the pitch on a full-size helicopter.

The American R/C "Rev-olution", the Kavan "Alouette 2", and the Schluter "Heli-Baby" are all designed to be "trainer" helicopters and they all take .40-cubic-inch displacement engines and four-channel radios. Most of them have optional features that can be added to give them aerobatic capabilities and "autorotation". These models sell for about $350 as kits, plus the cost of the engine ($100 to $200) and the four-channel radio rig. The American "Commander", Schluter "Heli-Boy", and the Kavan "Jet Ranger" are more advanced models that have true aerobatic capabilities. These aircraft require .60-cubic-inch displacement engines. The helicopter kits sell for about $600 and up, plus the cost of an engine and the radio rig. Most hobby shops that sell these models will have at least one customer who will assemble the helicopter kits for you, but this may be an expensive proposition! It might be worth it. A helicopter is the most precise model you can hope to build. Every single part must be aligned within a fraction of a degree with the next and assembled in a completely "fail-proof" manner, or the model will be unstable in flight. If you have assembled a dozen or more powered radio-control models and perhaps rebuilt an engine or two, you have nothing to fear from any of these kits. They're really not difficult to build—it's just that the nature of a helicopter allows virtually no room for error.

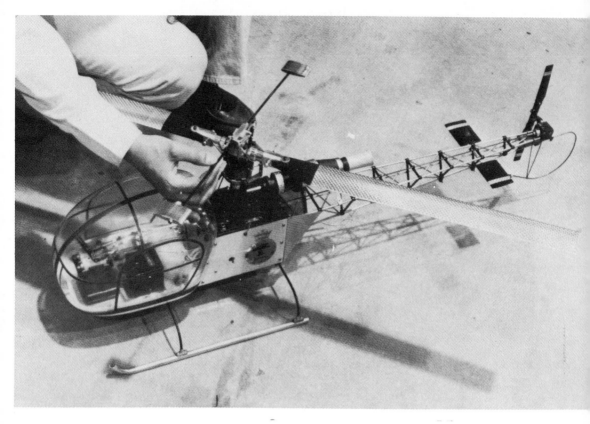

Fig. 8-7   The Kavan "Alouette 2" R/C helicopter is available as a beginner's kit and with enough options for aerobatic flight.

Autorotation

One of the major breakthroughs in model helicopter technology was the "autorotation" capability of some of the more expensive kits. This feature is sometimes an option on even the "trainer" models, and it's worth at least half the cost of the helicopter kit to get it. The "autorotation" option is nothing more than some form of an automatic clutch that will allow the main rotor to continue to revolve even if the engine is accidentally killed in flight or runs out of fuel. Without a clutch of some kind, the engine would soon stop the rotor, because the rotor would be trying to pull the engine around *against* its compression. Autorotation means a bit more than just a free-wheeling rotor, however.

A helicopter needs energy to fly just like a fixed-wing aircraft, and it has just about the same array of energy sources at the flier's disposal. If the engine dies at, say, a 100-foot elevation with the helicopter moving, say, five miles an hour, the flier has the energy of the 'craft's forward momentum, the energy of gravity pulling it down, and the rotational energy of the still-spinning rotors to use in helping to get the helicopter down to earth gently. The "trick" is to adjust the pitch of the main rotor blades so they will allow descent under "autorotation" to within five feet or so of the ground. Hopefully, there will still be enough energy left to allow the flier to adjust the rotor pitch for a slight amount of "lift" to be able to set the 'craft down gently. Obviously, autorotation relies on main rotors with adjustable pitch as much as it does on a clutch of some type. You must have both options on your model if you hope to be able to land it if the engine kills.

Helicopter Flight

The helicopter flies on its own lift. Unfortunately, the wind it creates is more of a bubble or dome. The difficulties with helicopter flight can, perhaps, be more apparent if you try to think of the helicopter's flying environment as a large dome of air. The rotor's angle from vertical, right or left, or fore and aft must be constantly adjusted to keep the helicopter in level flight. The adjustments for anything like a level hovering flight are even more delicate because there's no forward momentum to help stabilize the helicopter. That's what is meant by the statement that a helicopter, unlike a fixed-wing aircraft, really does not want to fly at all. The flier must make constant adjustments in the radio-control transmitter stick for right and left and fore and aft lean on the swash plate to keep the helicopter "balanced" on that "dome" of air in level flight. It's relatively simple to adjust the radio-control stick for engine speed to control the model's altitude, because that adjustment is not as delicate as that right/left and fore/aft balance.

Fig. 8-8   The basic Schluter "Heli-Boy" R/C helicopter can be modified into a scale model with this "Bell 222" body kit. *Courtesy Gorham Associates.*

The models that have rotors with pitch control are rigged with levers and control rods to provide what is known as "collective pitch". This simply means that both main rotors increase or decrease their angle or pitch at the same time. This helps to keep the rotor in balance and provides the precise control that is needed for aerobatic maneuvers. With practice, you can duplicate just about every maneuver an aerobatic fixed-wing aircraft can accomplish with a helicopter that has pitch control for the main rotor. Loops, figure eights, Immelmann turns, and even prolonged inverted flight and spiral dives are all *possible* with a radio-control helicopter. The most skillful radio-control fliers in the world are the guys and gals who can use their transmitters to perform aerobatics with a helicopter. If level hovering is difficult to balance, imagine what it must be like to maintain a perfect figure eight with those same controls.

Chapter 9
✈
Kit Building

The hobby aspect of the hobby/sport of flying model aircraft has gone through some changes that are as revolutionary as the new flying capabilities of modern radio-control rigs. The history of the hobby is filled with variations on the balsa rib, strut, and spar building techniques. Those types of kits are still predominant in the hobby, but the materials list in some kits now includes hard foam plastic wings and/or fuselages for really quick assembly, pre-shaped balsa fuselage surfaces and wings, vacuum-formed plastic sheet panels, and fiberglass fuselages and parts. There are several kits in virtually every category of model-aircraft types (except helicopters) that can be assembled in less than eight hours—including applying paint and any decals and trim. You still have to wait about 24 hours for most fuel-proof paints to dry completely, but you can even by-pass the paint step by covering the model with one of the pre-colored plastic sheet films like Top-Flite's "Super Monocote". The new kits, glues, and coverings can almost eliminate the hobby side of flying model aircraft completely for those who would really rather fly. Conversely, there are some truly challenging kits available that will reward the builder with an aircraft that really does fly better than any of the quick-build kits if he or she takes the time. Besides, almost all of the "stick model" kits from the forties and fifties are still available.

Cement Secrets
In our opinion, the old cellulose adhesives in a tube (like Duco "Household Cement" and a whole array of similar products from Ambroid, Testors and Duco) are virtually obsolete. Ambroid still remains the choice for most indoor free-flight models, however. Recent advances in the use of the cyanoacrylate adhesives like Eastman 910, Super Jet, Hot Stuff, and the like have made these almost instant-dry cements as versatile as cellulose glues used to be. It's our experience that these cyanoacrylates, white glue, aliphatic resin, regular epoxy, and five-minute epoxy are the best glues to use for building flying aircraft models. In fact, we strongly recommend that you purchase a small-size container of all five of these glues so you'll have them available for assembling the next kit. Keep them in the toolbox you take to the flying site for on-the-field repairs. You

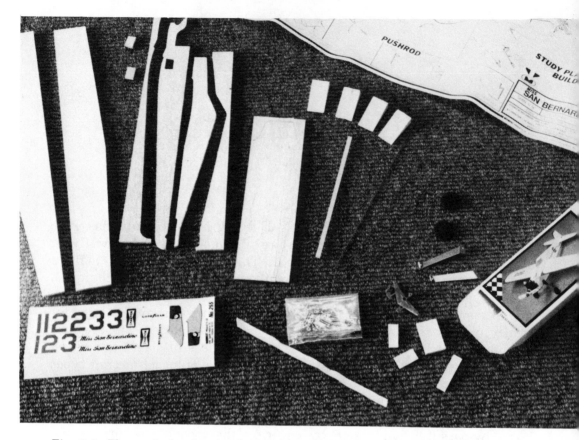

Fig. 9-1 The parts in the simple "profile" trainer kits, like Midwest's "Miss San Bernardino," are pre-cut for two-hour assembly.

can make your own decision as to whether you need both white glue and an aliphatic resin glue; they seem to have almost identical properties for assembling model aircraft, except that the aliphatic forms a slightly more flexible joint which is less likely to fracture, and it is a bit easier to sand. Regular-cure (30 minutes or more) epoxy will soak into the wood of a joint thanks to its overnight curing time, but the speed with which five-minute epoxy sets makes it useful for joints where you have to make repairs in the field. The epoxies are best for bonding metal to wood or plastic and for bonding metal to metal, metal to plastic, and plastic to plastic. Test them first on the foam type of plastic, because the heat that is generated during the cure or the chemical reaction can literally dissolve the foam! The white glue and/or aliphatic resin are the glues to use for joining wood to wood or foam plastic to foam plastic, if you can use a jig or pins to keep the parts in alignment until the glue dries. Sig "Core Bond" and other *water*-based contact cements are also good for gluing foam plastic.

Instant Glue Joints

The cyanoacrylate cements are, in our opinion, one of the greatest advances in model aircraft kit-building since the invention of the die-cut balsa ribs. The cyanoacrylate's odor is offensive to some, but some new brands on the market don't have quite as strong a smell. The cement is also relatively expensive, but a small bottle is usually enough to finish any kit with less than a five-foot wingspan. Its primary disadvantages are that it has a relatively short shelf life, particularly after being opened, and that it will glue your fingers just as tightly as anything else. The cement sets in a matter of seconds if the joint is airtight—and that's just the kind of joint you can get if you squeeze a glue-coated thumb and forefinger together. If you do make such a silly mistake, gently pull your fingers apart while you oh-so-carefully slice through the glue itself rather than your skin. You can increase the shelf life of the cement by keeping it in the refrigerator between building sessions if there are no small children in the house. Unopened bottles should be stored in the freezer until ready for use.

The cyanoacrylates rely on the absence of air to create a bond. If you are gluing two surfaces with a very tight fit together, a single drop of the cyanoacrylate cement should be enough. The cement will flow into the joint through capillary action. The age-old method of pinning the parts to the wax paper-covered plan with tee pins, hat pins, or common straight

Fig. 9-2 The "profile" models are fully aerobatic with fuselage and wing shapes similar to a full-size aircraft like Sterling's "Spitfire."

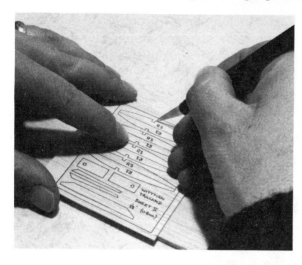

Fig. 9-3 Very few kits still require that you cut the wing ribs or fuselage bulkheads—most are die-cut to speed assembly.

Fig. 9-4 Full-size plans are included with free-flight kits. Cover them with wax paper and cut and glue right over the plans.

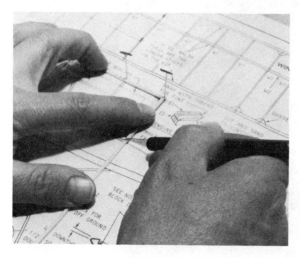

Fig. 9-5 Use tee pins to hold the wood while you cut the next piece to exact size right on the plans.

pins should be used so you don't glue your fingers (or tweezers) to the wood. For most such joints, that single drop of cyanoacrylate will be enough. The almost-magic aspect of the material is that you can glue joints and have them dry as rapidly as you can cut the stringers or spars. The model in the photographs is one of the "stick model" types that is still quite popular as "Peanut Scale" free-flight models.

The cyanoacrylate cement will not stick to wax paper, so use wax paper to cover any plans you are working with. A small square of wax paper can also be used to grip parts or to hold two parts together so you don't touch the parts with your fingers. One of the most important "tricks" to use when cementing with cyanoacrylate is to have a "filler" handy for those joints that are not quite perfect. Common baking soda makes a fine filler. Use a wood spatula or coffee stirring stick to apply the baking soda to the joint. A flat toothpick can be used to push the powder into place. A drop or two of cyanoacrylate is all that's needed to make the baking soda (at least) as tough as a white glue fillet. You can also build up fillets between the ribs and the spars with the baking soda and cyanoacrylate. Remember to add the cement to the baking soda, because the cement will set up hard in just a second or two. The cyanoacrylate cement can even be applied by punching a hole with a tee pin and flowing a drop or two of the cement into the hole so it will spread with capillary action.

Epoxies

Almost any brand of five-minute epoxy is suitable for assembling aircraft models. Epoxy is especially helpful where a great amount of strength is required and weight is not too great a problem. The epoxy will form its own fillet or radius where, for example, a wing rib joins the wing spar or wing surface panel. There is no need to add any type of filler material to the epoxy. It is much easier to form reinforcing fillets with five-minute epoxy than with the conventional epoxies. Conventional epoxies flow almost like water before they cure, so a large "pile" of epoxy will flow out into a tiny lake. You can work the five-minute types into a large-radius fillet right up to the time when they become gelatin-like. The five-minute epoxies have ample strength for the assembly of elevator, rudder, and fuselage joints. Joints that will receive extreme stress, like engine mounts and wing spars, should be installed with conventional epoxy because of their greater strength. If you need even greater strength, small pieces of fiberglass cloth (handle it with gloves) can be placed across the joint and the epoxy worked into the cloth. There is very little difference between the resin and catalyst used for fiberglass and epoxy, except that epoxy is thicker. The combination of fiberglass cloth and epoxy is essentially the same as the plastic-like material called "fiberglass". Please use caution and do keep your hands away from your eyes when working with epoxy, fiberglass cloth, and resin because the catalyst and cloth, in particular, are extremely dangerous.

Fig. 9-6 Cyanoacrylate cement can be applied to the wood joints while you hold the part in place for just a few seconds.

Fig. 9-7 Apply some baking soda to any joints that do not fit properly to fill in the gaps, then apply the cynoacrylate cement.

Fig. 9-8 Hold balsa wood covering panels in place with one hand while you use a tee pin to punch a hole through the wood with the other hand.

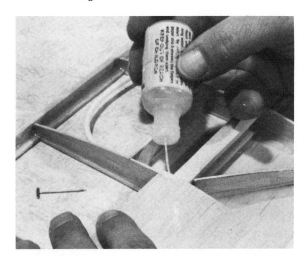

Fig. 9-9 A drop of cyanoacrylate cement, applied through that tee pin hole, will bond balsa wood covering to wing spars and ribs.

Fig. 9-10 Use regular-cure epoxy to assembled highly stressed parts to give the epoxy time to soak into the wood before it cures.

Fig. 9-11 You can form reinforcing "fillets" at the corners of parts that might break with five-minute epoxy.

Tools

Very few tools are required for the construction of most model aircraft kits, because the materials are all relatively soft woods or foam plastics. A good hobby knife like those sold by X-acto or Dixon is essential. The surgeon's scalpel type of hobby knife like an Uber Skiver is popular with those who work a lot with soft balsa wood kits. The X-acto Number 5 hobby knife handle is a good investment because it will accept X-acto razor saw blades, wood carving blades, and gouges or chisels. Pointed tweezers are another essential tool for any type of model aircraft work. We would suggest both the type that you squeeze to hold the part and the type that must be squeezed to release the part. A collection of about 50 each of small (straight pin-size), medium, and large (hat pin-size) tee pins will also be essential. The thin type of coffee-stirring wooden sticks are best for applying baking soda or epoxy. A collection of X-acto sanding blocks or simply hardwood blocks with sandpaper glued to them will take most of the work (and the sloppiness) out of sanding. Either Number 180 grit or fine-grain sandpaper is about right for most model airplane work.

Hardened steel music wire or piano wire is used for a number of things on many aircraft models, including parts like propeller hooks for free-flight models, landing gear, and tail wheel mounts and pushrods for both control-line and radio-control models. You'll ruin the best diagonal cutters trying to cut the stuff. Some large hardware stores sell special cutters, but most modelers use an abrasive cutoff wheel mounted in a motor tool like a Dremel. Be certain to wear safety glasses or goggles whenever you use a cutoff wheel, because the wheel will break once in a while. Strong needlenose pliers can be used to bend the piano wire.

There are some special tools that you may want to consider if you've decided that building flying model aircraft is going to be your hobby. The

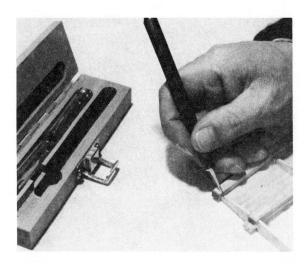

Fig. 9-12 A sharp hobby knife like this "Uber Skiver" will slice through balsa wood without chipping or crumbling the wood.

Fig. 9-13 An X-acto No. 5 handle with X-acto's router blades can be used to shape balsa blocks for wing tips, fairings, and cowls.

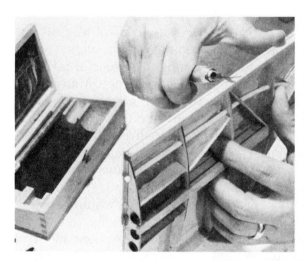

Fig. 9-14 The hook-shaped No. 28 blade in the No. 5 X-acto handle is best for carving the leading edges of wings.

Fig. 9-15 Glue some fine-grain sandpaper to a perfectly flat hardwood block to make your own sanding block.

special sealing irons sold for use with the plastic sheet coverings like "Monocote" are a must if you are going to use that type of covering for your aircraft models. A small sabre saw or jig saw is helpful for those who want to shape their own wing tips or cowls from blocks of balsa wood. The saw is also needed for cutting hardwood or plywood engine and radio-control servo mounting brackets. There are several really clever clamps and jigs to help align wing ribs and fuselage formers for those who like to build from plans and those who specialize in those large free-flight scale models. You will need a soldering iron for any wiring work on the radio-control kits, and the iron can prove helpful in making secure connections with piano wire for control rods and landing gear. You can use a common electric hand drill or even a hand-powered crank drill to drill the few holes that will be needed in the soft wood and plastic materials used in model aircraft construction.

Control Surfaces

The most critical parts of a control-line or radio-control aircraft are the hinged rudder, elevator, and ailerons. Some kits provide special nylon hinges that look like scale-model door hinges or special strips of flexible Mylar-type plastic tape that are to be used as a hinge. Many of the kits, however, assume that the builder will know all about making working hinges. At least a dozen firms make control hardware including hinges and the "control horns" that connect the pushrods from the bell crank lever (on a control-line model) or the servo motor wheels (on a radio-control model). Any store that stocks model airplane engines and piano wire and balsa should carry this type of hardware. It is also available by mail from firms like Sig and Ace R/C. We would strongly recommend that you obtain a catalog of this type of hardware so you can see the various types of hinges, control horns, and the assortment of hardware for the pushrods that is available. You can then decide which type of hardware will work best on your particular model. Figure 9-16 illustrates the use of the nylon "door" hinge buried inside the wing, rudder, or stabilizer (as it is designed to be) and the alternate method of utilizing a simple strip of flexible Mylar plastic tape. The alignment of the control horn holes over the hinge pivot point is particularly crucial. The hinges must also be in line with one another along the hinged edges of the flaps, and there must be ample room for the full movement of the flaps. This is the most critical part of assembling any control-line or radio-control model aircraft kit, so spend as much time as necessary to get the control surfaces working perfectly, without any slop or binding. Any drag placed on the servos by the binding action of faulty control surfaces will dramatically reduce the charge life of the batteries in the aircraft, and it may even damage the servos themselves.

CONVENTIONAL NYLON HINGE

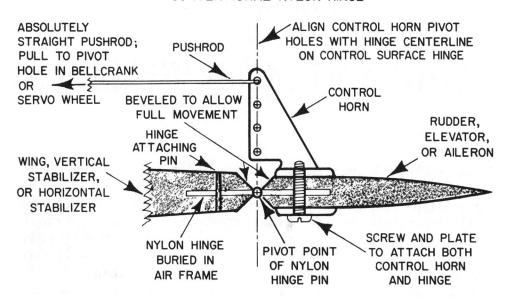

ABSOLUTELY
STRAIGHT PUSHROD;
PULL TO PIVOT
HOLE IN BELLCRANK
OR
SERVO WHEEL

PUSHROD

ALIGN CONTROL HORN PIVOT
HOLES WITH HINGE CENTERLINE
ON CONTROL SURFACE HINGE

CONTROL
HORN

BEVELED TO ALLOW
FULL MOVEMENT

RUDDER,
ELEVATOR,
OR AILERON

HINGE
ATTACHING
PIN

WING, VERTICAL
STABILIZER,
OR HORIZONTAL
STABILIZER

NYLON HINGE
BURIED IN
AIR FRAME

PIVOT POINT
OF NYLON
HINGE PIN

SCREW AND PLATE
TO ATTACH BOTH
CONTROL HORN
AND HINGE

PLASTIC TAPE HINGE

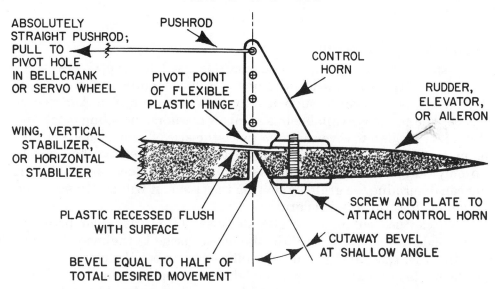

ABSOLUTELY
STRAIGHT PUSHROD;
PULL TO
PIVOT HOLE
IN BELLCRANK
OR SERVO WHEEL

PUSHROD

PIVOT POINT
OF FLEXIBLE
PLASTIC HINGE

CONTROL
HORN

RUDDER,
ELEVATOR,
OR AILERON

WING, VERTICAL
STABILIZER,
OR HORIZONTAL
STABILIZER

PLASTIC RECESSED FLUSH
WITH SURFACE

SCREW AND PLATE TO
ATTACH CONTROL HORN

CUTAWAY BEVEL
AT SHALLOW ANGLE

BEVEL EQUAL TO HALF OF
TOTAL DESIRED MOVEMENT

Fig. 9-16 The pivot holes for the pushrod ends (clevises) in the control horns must be aligned directly over the hinges for rudder, aileron, or elevator control surfaces to give perfect control response. The cutaway bevel can be a shallow angle, because half of the movement is upward—much smoother airflow with no air leakage. The flexible plastic tape hinge is almost unaffected by temperature or vibration.

Chapter 10

✦

Paint and Other Finishes

The days when a balsa wood or tissue-covered model was painted with Testor's "Dope" are now part of the history of the hobby. There are some improved types of fuel-proof paint that serve the same function that Dope used to. Japanese tissue paper is the best covering material *only* for most types of free-flight models. Most of the larger outdoor free-flight models, control-line models, and radio-control models that are built from kits are covered with some type of colored plastic sheet rather than paper and paint. The plastic can be repaired as easily as the tissue paper or painted balsa coverings, and it is both stronger and more durable. Since each type of covering has its unique advantages and applications, we'll describe them all.

Tissue Paper Covering

A special blend of paper and cloth is used for the tissue paper designed for covering model airplanes. It is generally referred to as "Japanese tissue", even though it may have been made in America or Europe. The tissue is available in a rainbow of colors, including black and white. Buy enough to cover an area twice the size of your model, because the material has a grain, and you'll waste a lot of it getting the grain to run only down the length of the fuselage, wings, rudder, and stablizer. You can determine the grain by tearing the tissue; it will tear easiest and straightest in the direction of grain.

You can use either white glue or Sig's "Lite-Coat" clear paint for flying model aircraft to "glue" the Japanese tissue to the model's structure. In either case, the fluid must be diluted by an equal amount of water (for the white glue) or Sig "Supercoat" thinner. Apply one light coat to the areas where the tissue will be attached to seal the wood and let it dry. The tissue must be applied to a single area at a time, so cut it into pieces at least an inch larger than, for example, the size of one wing. Coat the exterior edges of that wing with a second application of that 50/50 mix of "Lite-Coat" paint or white glue. You can use your fingertip to apply the white glue, because it will simply peel off when dry; use a paintbrush, however, for the "Lite-Coat". Stretch the tissue paper as tight as you can and pull it down and over the area. Rub over all the edges and ribs with

Fig. 10-1   Use white glue (or aliphatic resin glue) thinned with an equal amount of water to hold Japanese tissue to the aircraft's frame.

your finger to stick the tissue firmly and set that panel aside to dry for a few hours. You can then move on to the other wing, the top of the stabilizer, the rudder, and one side of the fuselage. When each has dried completely, trim off the excess paper with a hobby knife. Finally, sand the edges of paper even with the edge of the model. You can now apply the tissue to the remaining areas, let it dry, and cut and sand its edges to completely cover the model.

The tissue must be stretched taut over the model by spraying it with a soft mist of water or rubbing alcohol and letting the tissue dry. Spray the water on the wings, rudder, and stabilizer while they are sill separate from the fuselage so you can pin these parts down while the water evaporates to prevent any warpage. Spray just one side of each wing, rudder, and stabilizer, pin the parts down, and let them dry before doing the same thing to the opposite side. The hand-pump spray bottles used for hair setting fluids or for misting house plants will work fine for this job.

Most modelers who fly indoor free flight with the tissue-covered models don't paint the tissue, because they don't want the added weight. In fact, these types of flying models should be decorated with tissue paper rather than decals for any license or I.D. numbers or stripes. You can cut such markings from colored tissue by sandwiching the tissue between ten pages or so of an old telephone book so the pages hold the tissue flat. Cut right through the pages and the tissue with a sharp hobby knife to make individual letters, numbers, or stripes. Spray them with a mixture of

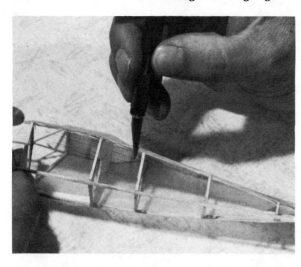

Fig. 10-2 When the glue dries, the oversize piece of tissue can be trimmed along the aircraft's frame with a sharp hobby knife.

50/50 white glue and water, then place them on the model with tweezers. If you want to protect the tissue on a free-flight model that will be flown outdoors, use that mixture of Sig "Lite-Coat" clear paint and thinner. The same pump-type sprayer that was used for the water can be used for the paint if you clean it thoroughly with pure thinner when you are done. Be sure to use clear paint, because it weighs much less than the colored paints. The rudder, stabilizer, and wings should be sprayed one side at a time, as described for the tissue-shrinking operation, and held to a flat board with pins so they don't warp. The black panel lines for the control flap hinges and the lines around doors or cowls can be applied with a fine-point felt-tip pen.

Plastic Color Coverings

The application techniques for the flexible plastic sheet or film coverings like Top-Flite's "Super Monocote," "Econocote" (with a low-

Fig. 10-3 If you can reach the *back* edge (as you can with wings, rudder, and stabilizer), use a sanding block to remove excess tissue.

temperature adhesive for plastic foam models), Pactra's "Solar Film," or Polk's "Wing skin" are very similar. There are some important variations in the application sequence, however, so be sure to read the instructions furnished with the roll. Most of these are available in a wide range of colors that are either totally opaque (solid colors) or slightly translucent (see-through). You can use the coverings over an open-frame model in a manner similar to Japanese tissue or in place of paint over a balsa wood or plastic foam model. The plastic film weighs only about a third what a smooth fuel-proof paint finish weighs, and it's far easier to apply. There will still be small detail areas like landing gear doors, wing tip fuel tanks, and sharply rounded engine cowls where fuel-proof paint must be used. The plastic films can be painted with special fuel-proof paints for camouflage effects and other special markings. Decals can be applied directly to the plastic films if the decals are protected with a final coat of clear fuel-proof paint. They say you can use a conventional clothes iron to heat and bond and shrink the plastic coverings, but don't bother. The weight and heat control of such irons make them impractical. If you are going to use the plastic coatings, invest in one of the special modeler's

Fig. 10-4   Buy one of the special irons (bottom) to heat and seal any of the special plastic model aircraft coverings like "Super Monocote".

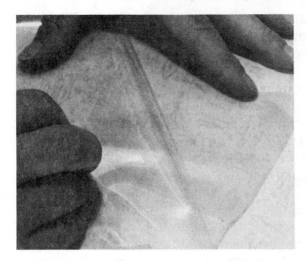

Fig. 10-5 Cut a piece of "Super Monocote" plastic film a bit larger than the wing or other area you are covering. Peel the backing from the adhesive side of the plastic film.

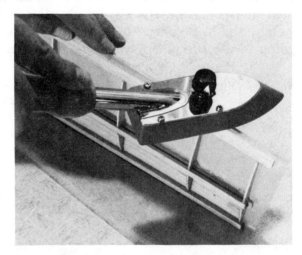

Fig. 10-6 Place the plastic film over the top of the wing, adhesive side down, and seal it on the trailing edge of the wing. Stretch the plastic film taut and heat seal it on the leading edge, then trim the excess away.

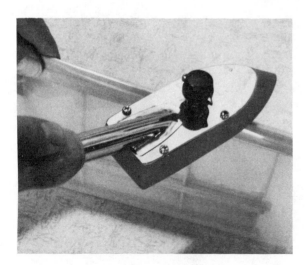

Fig. 10-7 Attach the bottom piece of plastic film so it overlaps the top piece on the leading and trailing edges of the wing by about ⅛ inch.

Fig. 10-8 Remove the excess material from the covering on the bottom of the wing with a sharp hobby knife. Try to cut only through that second layer of plastic film, not into the wood itself.

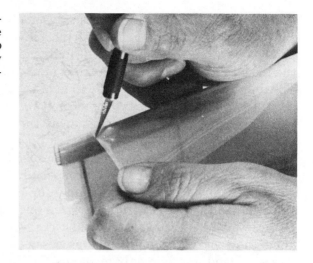

irons that are designed for only this use. A heat gun (a modified type of hair dryer) is a luxury you won't need unless you're building a model for "scale or "finish" contests.

The plastic films will adhere either to the wood frame of the model or to themselves. It's easier to obtain a neat finish if you bond the material to the edges of the wings, rudder, and stabilizer before these items are assembled to the fuselage. The iron's heat should be adjusted so it is hot enough to soften the plastic film but cool enough so it doesn't drag or catch as you pull it over the surface. It will take some experimenting with scraps of plastic and balsa to get it precisely right. The sequence is simple enough: Seal the plastic film along one edge of the panel, pull the film taut, and seal the opposite edge. Use a sharp hobby knife to trim the excess material away. Repeat the procedure immediately with the opposite side and overlap the plastic film over the edges of the first side by at

Fig. 10-9 Hold the iron about ¼ to ½ inch from the plastic film to heat the film so it will shrink enough to remove any trace of wrinkle.

least ⅛-inch. When all the edges are sealed with the iron, move the iron slowly over the entire surface of the plastic film to shrink it. You may need to punch a few pinholes through the edges of the wood to ventilate the model if the plastic film balloons outward rather than shrinking tight. The only way to know how close to hold the iron and how fast to move it to shrink away the wrinkles without melting the plastic film is to practice. If you make a mistake, simply trim away the film from that side of the panel and try again.

The plastic film coverings can be used to build in wing warp for a "wash-in" or "wash-out" effect for special flight trim or to help work out an accidental warp in a wing, rudder, or stabilizer. Simply hold the warp you want in the panel while you skim over the surface to smooth out the wrinkles you've made in the plastic covering. When the wrinkles are gone, the warp will remain. The process is a whole lot easier if you have a helper to add another pair of hands. In fact, the whole plastic-covering process itself is easier and a neater model will result if you have someone to help.

Painting Techniques

It is essential that fuel-proof paint be used on any model aircraft that will be powered by a fuel-burning engine. Since these paints are designed for easy use on balsa and tissue, they're good ones to choose even for a rubber-powered model or a sailplane. Special fuel-proof paints are available for use on foam plastic surfaces. At least one coat of sanding sealer must be used to fill in the grain on wood surfaces. Sand that first coat and all but the last color coat with Number 400 wet-or-dry sandpaper dipped frequently in water. Wipe the model clean, after each sanding, with a damp paper towel and dry it thoroughly. The smoothness of the fininsh will depend on how much sanding you must do between coats of

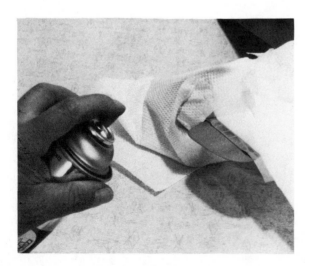

Fig. 10-10 Use Scotch "Magic" tape to mask the edges of any two-color areas. Tape paper towels to the model to mask near the area.

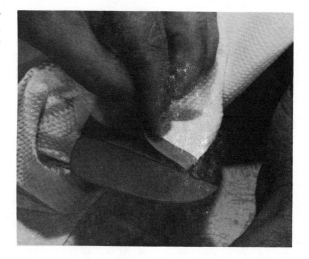

Fig. 10-11 Spray the second color and let it dry for only about an hour before peeling back the Scotch "magic" tape.

paint. You can obtain a smoother finish, with less work, if you use a sanding block (see Fig. 10-3). If you're building a true-scale aircraft that will have an engine with plenty of power, you may want as many as four coats of sanding sealer and a half-dozen coats of color. A free-flight model or glider should have a total of only two or three coats, to keep the weight as low as possible. Most of these paints are available in either bottles or aerosol cans, so you can pick the method of application that you feel most comfortable with.

Decal Markings

You can improve the appearance of almost any model aircraft by adding some type of decals, even if only to simulate an imaginary I.D. or your AMA number. Some model shops carry decals that have a removable paper backing with a sticky surface that is merely pressed onto the

Fig. 10-12 Hobby shops and drafting supply stores sell stripping tape that can be simply pressed on the model to simulate hinges or to make stripes.

Fig. 10-13 Cut the decals into individual numbers or letters with scissors. Hold the decal with tweezers and dip it into water for a minute.

Fig. 10-14 Let the decal glue dissolve on a paper towel. When the decal is free, hold the decal and paper on the model with a knife tip while you pull the decal paper backing away with tweezers.

Fig. 10-15 Gently dab at the decal with a damp facial tissue wrapped around your fingertip to push out any bubbles and to force the decal over details.

model's surface. Most of the markings you'll want will probably be available only as "wet" decals. The application sequence for applying decals with water-soluble glue is simple enough, but you must follow it exactly to obtain a proper decal finish: Cut the decal and the paper backing close to the colored portion of the decal. Hold the decals with tweezers and a knife blade tip from now on. Dip the decal into warm water for a few seconds, then set it on a paper towel for about two to five minutes while the water has a chance to soak through the paper backing and to dissolve the glue. When the decal is free to move on its paper backing, position both the decal and the paper where you want the decal. Hold the decal with a knife blade tip while you pull the paper backing from beneath it with tweezers. Dab the decal lightly with a paper towel or facial tissue wrapped tightly around your finger to "set" the decal on the surface. When the decal has dried overnight, spray it lightly with clear fuel-proof paint to seal it.

Repair Tips

If you fly a model aircraft, you will eventually crash it. Even the experts are fooled by weather conditions or mechanical failures. There are very few crashes so severe that the model cannot be repaired with modern cements and coverings. The most important part of any repair begins right after the crash; you must retrieve all of the pieces no matter how mangled they may seem. If you have them all, then the repair becomes little more than a three-dimensional jigsaw puzzle with the pieces held in place with five-minute epoxy or cyanoacrylate cement. A few clamps and some wax paper will help hold some of the parts in alignment while you epoxy the broken wood (or white glue the foam plastic) back together. If the surface was covered with one of the plastic films, simply cut the plastic film back to the nearest intact rib or spar. Fix the internal fractures with

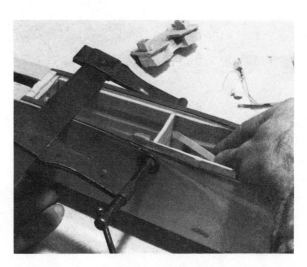

Fig. 10-16 You can repair some really terrible crash damage if you remember to save all the pieces. Clamp the parts while slow-cure epoxy cures.

Fig. 10-17 Remove the "Super Monocote" type of plastic film (or tissue paper) covering from over any areas with internal damage.

Fig. 10-18 Cement any broken balsa wood parts back together with the cyanoacrylate cement. Use baking soda if needed for "filler".

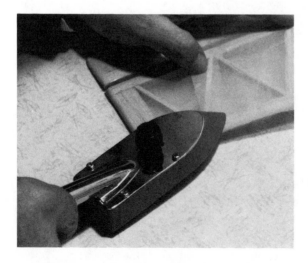

Fig. 10-19 Cut a piece of "Super Monocote" (if that was the original covering) about ¼-inch larger than the "patch". Bond it and heat-shrink in place, then trim away any excess.

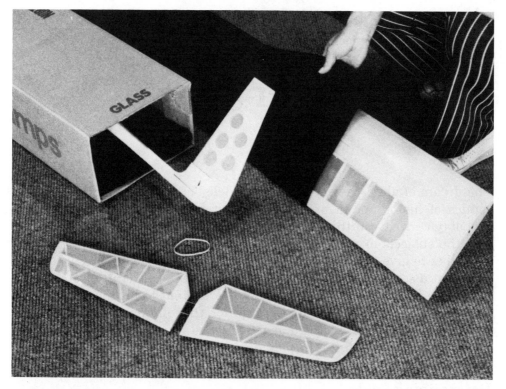

Fig. 10-20 Most model aircraft damage occurs on the way to and from the flying site. You can minimize it by making soft cloth bags for the parts; use a box to protect the model.

cement, then cut a piece of plastic film to cover the hole and heat-shrink it in place. If the model was painted, the plastic film can often be used to cover the entire area so it will act both as a fresh covering for color and as an external reinforcement for the model.

Showroom-Fresh Tips

The fuel-proof paints and the plastic films have made it far easier for a modeler to keep his or her aircraft looking brand-new. You can wipe away most dirt with a damp rag or with a bit of liquid kitchen cleaner like "Formula 409". You can prevent the most common cause of model damage by making a packing crate to house the model on its way to and from the flying site. The cardboard cartons that fluorescent tubes are packed in make fine crates for most models. Make a bag for the wings and fuselage from corduroy cloth with the fuzzy side in so the pieces of the aircraft won't bang against each other inside the carton.

Chapter 11

✈

Super Scale

The dream of almost every aircraft modeler is to build and fly a perfect replica of his or her favorite full-size aircraft. That's the fantasy that probably carried you this far through this book. Scale flying models are also the subjects of more broken dreams than any other type of model. We'd like to give you the benefit of thousands of modelers' experience: If you want a scale model of some particular "dream" aircraft or other, buy one of the static model plastic kits and be content to let the thing sit on your bookshelf. If you still have to go for that dream, then how about building your second or third most favorite aircraft? There's a better chance, then, that you might pick one that will fly as nicely as a model built from one of those $15 basic "trainer" kits.

Determining Scale

This is a good place to get the concept of a scale model into the proper perspective. The term "scale" refers to the proportions of the model as compared to the proportions of the real thing. Scale is usually expressed as a fraction but it is also a ratio. A $1/48$-scale model is the same as a 1 : 48-scale model; either one is precisely 48 times smaller than the real aircraft: every detail and line of the model is $1/48$ the size of the real aircraft, right down to the diameter of the landing wheels and tires and the thickness of the frames around the canopy or cockpit. The size of the fraction will give you a fair idea of the size of the model; a $1/24$-scale model is only half the size of a $1/12$-scale model. We say "fair idea" because the scale fractions indicate only the relative size of the linear dimensions of the model as compared to the full-size aircraft. That $1/12$-scale model will occupy four times the floor space of the $1/24$-scale version and eight times the cubic area. A $1/4$-scale model doesn't sound all that large until you view it in three-dimensional reality.

Scale Performance

The cubic size of a scale model brings us a bit closer to why you might have problems trying to fly a scale model of many full-size aircraft. A flying model must push aside the same air as the full-size aircraft did, but there's no way to reduce the effect of that air to match the size of the model. There's also no way to scale down gravity and the other forces of

Fig. 11-1 Royal Products' "stand-off scale" model of Lucky Lindy's famous aircraft hides the model engine beneath the cowl. *Courtesy Royal Products.*

Fig. 11-2 Peck-Polymer's "Nesmith Cougar" is a peanut scale free-flight kit that is popular with indoor fliers. *Courtesy Peck-Polymers.*

Fig. 11-3 The pilot in this peanut-scale P-51 Mustang is really a peanut shell. The model
is covered with silver-colored tissue.

nature that affect a flying aircraft, whether it be what we call "full-size"
or a model. The one dimension that we don't care about reducing to exact
scale is weight—"all" we expect is that the model perform in a manner
similar to the full-size aircraft. That's the criterion that's used for judging
scale models in most of the outdoor flying scale contests, too. It's seldom
that easy, for most "scale" model aircraft *must* fly faster than the real
thing just to remain airborne without stalling. That's because the air is so
"thick" and gravity is so strong relative to the "world" of the model. The
problem is even more pronounced when the aircraft we love has two or
more engines.

You probably haven't even considered entering that scale model of
your own "dream" aircraft in any contests. Just seeing a model like that in
the air would seem to be reward enough for building it. The facts are
never quite that simple, either; you'll join the ranks of the rest of us scale
modelers when that dream ship is complete and expect it to fly like the
real thing. If it comes even close, you"ll wonder how well it would do when
compared to the appearance and flying ability of the other scale models
you see here and in the monthly model aircraft magazines. It's too late to
make any really effective changes in the performance of the model after it
is built, but there are a number of things you can do while you're still
searching for the best way to make that dream into a scale model reality
in three dimensions.

The Scale Effect

By now you should be ready for a fact of flying: The larger the scale of the model, the closer it will come to the performance of the real thing. That's one of the reasons why ¹/₄-scale models are becoming more and more popular. You cannot model any old aircraft in ¹/₄ scale—a B-29 bomber would be as large as most for-real private planes—but you can pick a prototype that was a relatively small aircraft for your model. That's one of the reasons why World War I aircraft are so popular as ¹/₄-scale aircraft and why a tiny biplane like the Pitts makes such a fine subject or a ¹/₃-scale model. The closer you can get to making the model large enough to match the real-world effects of gravity and air density, the closer the model will be to the performance of its prototype.

Larger aircraft models require larger engines, and that alone is enough to scare some people. Once you get above a .60-cubic-inch engine, however, the cost doesn't change much all the way up to the 2.5-cubic-inch engine thumpers that are popular with ¹/₄-scale radio-control fliers. A multi-cylinder engine or a Wankel will be costly, but there's no particular reason why you should use a complex power plant when a simple one will do the job. The effect of scale applies almost inversely to the materials used for a model aircraft; your model is likely to be several times stronger than the real thing. The strength of the materials will also allow you to build a large scale model that is quite light. That means that the extra weight of radio-control gear won't have much effect on the model's performance. It will also mean that the model will stand a better chance of

Fig. 11-4   This Flyline Models free-flight "Velie Monocoupe" model has been fitted with Hungerford (Peck-Polymers) real wire wheels for extra realism.

Fig. 11-5   Royal Products offers many of their models in two different sizes. This Cessna 182 kit is available with either a 56- or 72½-inch wingspan. *Courtesy Royal Products.*

Fig. 11-6   This Guillow brand P-47 "Thunderbolt" has been left in an unfinished state on the right wing to show its construction of balsa wood with plastic detail parts. *Courtesy Paul K. Guillow, Inc.*

surviving a crash without any terminal damage. The scale models in the smaller scales (say, smaller than $1/18$ scale for a World War I model or $1/24$ for a slightly larger prototype) result in relatively heavy models that have a greater chance of breaking to bits on impact. We'll end this plea for sensibility in a choice of prototypes for your dream machine model by recommending that you also try to find a kit (rather than building from plans) and that the kit be as large a scale as you can find, regardless of cost.

Cheap Scale

If you feel that a large-size flying scale model is too far beyond your budget, we suggest you look at the other end of the scale spectrum—the indoor flying scale models. These are also known as "peanut scale" or "jumbo scale", depending on the wingspan. We discussed them back in Chapter 7 as part of the free-flight category of flying models. These models are fairly inexpensive kits and a big step up from a plastic shelf model. Almost all the free-flight scale models, however, are what used to be called "stick models", so they do require a whole lot of patience to assemble and even more to assemble well enough so they'll actually fly. These models are not expected to fly anywhere near as well as the full-size prototypes for the simple reason that the flier has virtually no control over them once they are launched. There are kits or plans for just about any propeller-driven aircraft you could imagine.

Control-Line Scale

The control-line models are one of the most practical ways to fulfill that dream of building your favorite aircraft and flying it as a scale model. The standard limitations of control-line flying are part of the deal, but you may not care whether or not your "dream" has two strings attached to it. There are dozens of ready-to-fly models and simple snap-together "one-hour" kits available as control-line models from firms like Cox and Testors in America and from some Japanese and European firms. You may find the model of your dreams almost ready-to-fly for less than $15. Don't overlook the hundreds of balsa wood kits for control-line scale models, either. Most of them sell for less than $50, and that's less than half of what a large-scale radio-control flying scale model will sell for as a kit. Some of the "stand-off" scale control-line models capture the overall appearance of the favorite full-size aircraft with just enough modifications to the wing area and stabilizer to make them fly well.

Radio-Control Scale

Radio control is usually part of that same "dream" of building and flying a model of your favorite full-size aircraft. After all, if you're going to dream, why not include the control system that allows the most realistic flight, including every imaginable prototype maneuver? In fact, there are

Fig. 11-7 This P-38L "Lightning" has a 40-inch wingspan. It's a Guillow kit that is adaptable to R/C, control line, or free flight. *Courtesy Paul K. Guillow, Inc.*

Fig. 11-8 This "Libelle" sailplane was built from a Soarcraft kit by Matt Sheldon. It has a 119-inch wingspan.

almost as many large-scale models designed for radio control as there are in any other model aircraft control category. Dozens of small firms (and some pretty large ones) make kits for exact-scale aircraft models. Many of them feature pre-formed balsa wood sheet or fiberglass fuselages and wings to make the shaping part of the kit easier. Very few of these models (or any other scale kits, for that matter) actually mention their exact scale. If you really care, you'll have to know enough about the full-size aircraft to translate its wingspan into that given for the model kit. Many of these kits include the materials, at least, for a fully detailed interior. There are also hundreds of accessories, from scale-size dummy engines to instruments to seat belts, for those who want to carry the appearance of reality to the ultimate.

A radio-control aircraft model with about a six-foot wingspan is a pretty serious piece of modeling. That's a typical size for most of the radio-control flying scale models. By the time you buy an engine large enough to fly the model and the radio rig, you'll have invested well over $500 and maybe more than $1,000. Maybe, just maybe, you should consider "shelving" that dream for long enough so you can learn to fly radio-control aircraft. When you've built that fifth or sixth radio-control

Fig. 11-9   Proper paint and decals make this Guillow model of the Focke-Wulf Fw190 appear almost exactly like the prototype. *Courtesy Paul K. Guillow, Inc.*

kit and you know it will fly when you walk out to the field the first time, you're ready to take on the task of adding the problems of scale-size wings and stabilizers and rudders to your hobby. That scale radio-control aircraft will weigh about half again as much as the radio-control "pattern" or "sport" models you've built and/or it will be twice as big. It's certainly not the kind of model that anybody would recommend as a "trainer". We don't want to discourage you, but we would like to prevent that dream from becoming a nightmare.

Chapter 12

Clubs and Competition

Flying really is more fun when you share it with someone. You cannot take a passenger up with you on those flights, but you certainly can find a few hundred thousand other modelers who may have shared the same thrills and the same disappointments. There are radio-control flying clubs in virtually every town in America and in every major city of the world. There are almost as many clubs who favor control-line models. Yes, you may have to search a bit for a group who wants to fly nothing but free-flight or radio-control helicopters, but those groups are active in every major city. Each of those thousands of clubs has its own flying field, and most of them hold regular contests. There are also several state contests, as well as annual national and international meets. Even if you are not interested in competing just yet, the members of the clubs have the information you need to make the hobby/sport more fun at every level. Those guys and gals are the ones who truly do know what you're talking about when you want to share the feeling of flying.

Local Clubs

The salespeople in the hobby shops in your area will be able to tell you how to contact the nearby clubs. There are generally regular monthly meetings, and most of the training of new fliers is accomplished in short sessions at the flying field if the weather is good. If the weather is bad, many clubs hold indoor meetings where flying films of both full-size and model aircraft of interest appear. Try to remember, when you attend the meetings, that the club is not an extension of the hobby shop; none of the members has any reason whatsoever to feel indebted to you for showing up to ask for help. None of the members was born with a control handle or radio transmitter in his or her hand, either. There are always a few folk at the meeting who still remember what it was like to be a new modeler or flier, and they're most willing to help. You can do your part by being polite and patient until you find a moment or two when one or more of the members can devote some attention to you. In the meantime, you can just soak up the "buzz" words and the general aura of kindred souls at play. It's your responsibility to find out what the club rules may be and what you have to do to be able to fly at the club's field. The field may be on

Fig. 12-1 Participants in a Rocky Mountain Soaring Association sailplane meet will gain valuable flying experience when they compare their skills to those of the other club members.

private property, but it's no different from a baseball field; you may have to wait your turn to fly, and you most certainly will have to follow certain safety and courtesy rules.

Academy of Model Aeronautics

Your local flying club will probably be chartered by the Academy of Model Aeronautics (AMA), the American organization of flying aircraft enthusiasts. There are similar organizations in almost every other country of the world. Each of the local club members is also a member of the AMA. The organization includes more than 70,000 active members, about 10 percent of them under the age of 19. The AMA is America's representative in the Fédération Aéronautique Internationale (FAI), the international governing body for the hobby/sport. The AMA sponsors annual national contests (called "the NATS") at different locations in the country. The FAI sponsors world championships, and several of those have been held in America over the years. Membership in the AMA includes liability insurance while you fly your models, the annual AMA rule book, and a monthly model airplane magazine *Model Aviation* with how-to articles, contest reports, new product information, and news about the organization. Official AMA-sanctioned events (and AMA members) are covered by a million dollars in liability insurance. The full information packet on AMA membership is available from the Academy of Model Aeronautics, 1810 Samuel Morse Dr., Reston, VA 22090.

National Model Airplane Championships

The National Model Airplane Championships is a combination of the excitement of a baseball World Series and a circus. The "NATS" is the annual gathering of the faithful where the most realistic scale models in the world are flown by people who make them perform precisely like the real thing. Activities of the twelve different classes of radio-control, control-line, and free-flight scale model aircraft are just a fraction of what goes on during NATS week near the end of July and early August. There are sixteen classes of free-flight events for both indoor and outdoor competition, fourteen control-line events, ten radio-control events, fifteen for FAI or world championship classes, and another ten for the affiliated Society of Antique Modelers aircraft. The SAM models are those built from plans published prior to December 31, 1938, including gliders and both internal combustion engine-powered and rubber-powered models; all of the free-flight type. You'll see every imaginable type of flying model aircraft at the NATS, including some examples whose designs date back

Fig. 12-2 The paraphernalia of an avid indoor scale free-flight competitor includes his model's score sheet, a commercial propeller winding machine, a razor blade, rubber lube, and coffee (for the flier).

to the beginnings of the hobby. The individual classes are listed and defined in the AMA rulebook that covers everything but rockets. The rockets people have the National Association of Rocketry (NAR) with their own rules and their own championships.

Almost every flier at the NATS belongs to one of the clubs affiliated with the AMA. Most of these clubs have their own championships, but they are usually for just one category of aircraft (like free flight). The NATS is the place where you see everything there is to see in the hobby in one place. Thousands of people plan their vacations around the NATS, however, so be sure to make room or camping reservations in advance if you do plan to attend. The site of the next year's event is not usually decided until the week of the current year's event, and it is then published in the AMA's *Model Aviation* magazine as well as in many of the other monthly model aircraft magazines. Many of the AMA-affiliated clubs have championships of their own, with the winner or winners being given expense-paid trips to the NATS. The very best fliers in this country attend the NATS, even if they have to pay their own way there. The rules do not limit the number of entries, however, so there is no reason why you cannot at least enter the events you have aircraft to qualify for. You do, of course, need to be an AMA member, but you'll need to join just to get your copy of the rulebook in any case. More than one AMA champion has been a guy or gal who just "showed up".

Fig. 12-3   One of the areas of judging for some types of sailplane competition is the flier's ability to land in the center of a circle. This competitor is just about to do it!

Fig. 12-4   Ray Marvin is launching his Unlimited Class sailplane at a Rocky Mountain Soaring Association meet. The two men in the background are flying (right) and judging (left) a previous launch.

The Rules

The current AMA rulebook has 98 pages of text and illustrations, so we cannot begin to reproduce it all here. There are classes for events and types of model aircraft like all of those you see in this book, and there are some, like speed, "Navy Carrier", "Dive Bombing & Strafing", and "Pylon Racing" that are too advanced for this type of book. The rulebook specifies the allowable wingspans, engines sizes (if any), weights, and general shapes, as well as how the flights themselves will be judged. Those same rules are, obviously, the ones that most of the local clubs use for their competition events. The rulebook also includes a number of safety precautions (in addition to the general safety rules shown in Chapter 1 of this book) for high-speed and heavy control-line models. The section on scale will give you some fine pointers on how to build a scale model that will meet the standards by which the AMA judges such models for both appearance and flying ability. Anyone contemplating the construction of a scale model, whether for competition or not, should first study the AMA rulebook. The typical stunt maneuvers for both control-

Fig. 12-5 This Sig "Mustang Stunter" is typical of the aircraft that compete in the aerobatics of the control-line stunt classes at various AMA club and national events. *Courtesy Sig Manufacturing Co., Inc.*

Fig. 12-6   A simulated aircraft carrier deck is used for some of the AMA control-line events. Some models even have arresting hooks to catch lines strung across the forward end of the "deck."

Fig. 12-7   This simple-to-build Sig brand "profile" model "Twister" has all of the controls (including adjustable wing flaps) that are needed for "control-line stunt" competition flying. *Courtesy Sig Manufacturing Co., Inc.*

line and radio-control models will give experienced fliers an idea of what "pattern" maneuvers really can be.

Each of the rules for competitive AMA flying is proposed and voted on by the contest board for that segment of the hobby/sport. Free-flight rules are the products of the experience of members with free-flight experience, radio-control rules are the result of the R/C members, experience, and so forth. These contest board members are also members of local AMA-affiliated clubs who very likely fly only the types of aircraft that are the specialty of that board member. The AMA rules are, then, both proven and practical means of judging the best performance of both the aircraft model and the flier. The rules are printed in the AMA rulebook and used by virtually every model aircraft club in the country. This greatly simplifies the technical operation of any local contest.

When you join an AMA-affiliated model aircraft club, you also benefit from the experience of the hundreds of thousands of fliers who have helped develop AMA rules and contest formats. The contests are certainly *not* the basis for the hobby of flying model aircraft; in fact, quite the

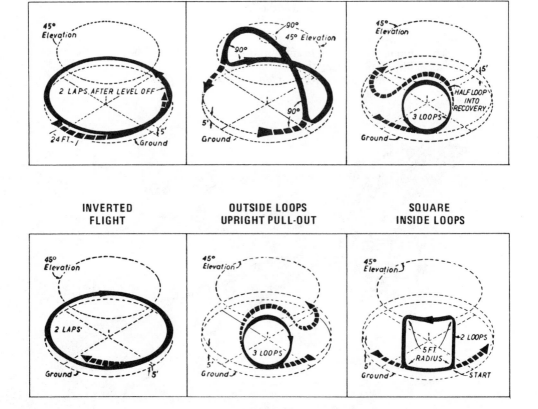

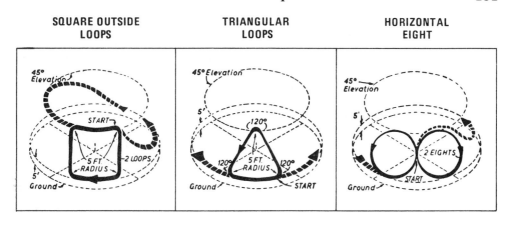

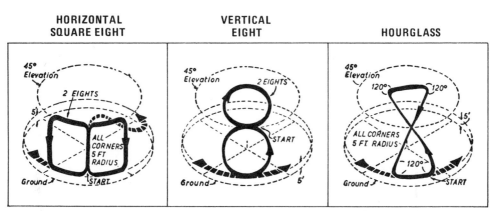

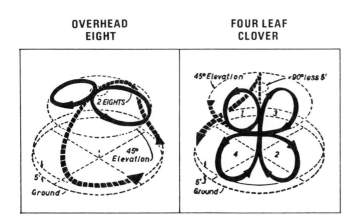

Fig. 12-8 Fourteen examples of the type of "precision aerobatics" that are performed by most of the successful competitors in control-line "Stunt" flying classes at AMA events. *Courtesy Cox Hobbies.*

reverse is true—the contests grew out of the hobby. The contests will, though, give you some added stimulation to improve both your construction and flying abilities for your own satisfaction. There's really no substitute for a personal learning experience of the type you'll receive when you enter a contest and discover just why other aircraft may (or may not) fly better than your own. The flight or sport side of aircraft modeling is something that takes some time to learn. You can minimize that learning period by drawing on the experience of other fliers to help you learn by example rather than by trail and error. Besides, you'll have fun!

Glossary

Aerobatics: Flying aircraft maneuvers, like loops and rolls, that are not needed for normal transportation flights.

Aerodynamics: The study of machines and objects moving in air.

Ailerons: The control surfaces or flaps pivoted from the rear of an aircraft's wings to help control roll.

Airfoil: The cross-sectional shape of a wing or other flying surface.

Airframe: The form that gives a flying machine its shape and strength, including the interior portions of wings and fuselages.

Aliphatic resin: One of the types of liquid glues used to assemble wood or plastic aircraft models. Sold under various trade names.

AMA: The Academy of Model Aeronautics; the major American flying model aircraft organization.

Angle of attack: The angle, in degrees, included between the bottom of an airfoil (or the centerline of a "symmetrical airfoil") and the directional path of flight.

Aspect ratio: The numerical ratio of a wing's chord divided into the wingspan.

Average chord: The total area of the wing divided by the wingspan.

Balsa wood: A lightweight but strong wood that is easily cut.

Bearers: Plywood or hardwood brackets used to mount radio-control servos in the fuselage.

Brick: A form of radio-control unit where the receiver and two or more servo motors are built into a single housing.

Canard: A type of aircraft design where the wing is at the rear of the aircraft with the "stabilizer" at the front.

Center of gravity: See *CG.*

Center of Pressure: The single point on a wing or other airfoil where all of the lifting forces are centered.

CG: Center of gravity; the point where all the masses or weight of the aircraft are centered. Also, the balance point of the model in any plane or direction.

Channel: A single function of a radio-control system.

Chord: The width of a wing or other airfoil.

Decal: A thin decoration, number, letter, or stripe to be applied to the surface of a model.

Decalage: The angle of difference between the wing and the stabilizer as viewed from the side of the aircraft.

Digital proportional: See *Fully Proportional.*

Dihedral: The upward or downward angle of a wing or other airfoil when viewed from the front of the aircraft.

Doublers: An extra layer of wood used to reinforce a fuselage, usually at the point where the wing mounts to the fuselage.

Drag: The retarding action of an object that results from the air stream's resistance to flowing smoothly over the surface.

Elevator: The control surface that is pivoted from the rear of the horizontal stabilizer.

Elevon: The control surfaces that are pivoted from the rear of the wings of a delta-winged (triangular-shaped) aircraft. Elevons control both pitch and roll simultaneously because each is a combination elevator and rudder in one control surface.

Empennage: Collectively, the rudder and stabilizer or any other control surfaces at the rear of the aircraft.

FAI: Fédération Aéronautique Internationale; the organization governing both model and full-size aircraft competition world-wide.

FCC: The Federal Communications Commission; the licensing body of the government that assigns radio frequencies and controls their use.

Fin: A vertical surface that helps to provide directional control.

Flaps: The movable control surfaces at the rear of an airfoil that are used to control the aircraft's lift or stability.

Flutter: The low-frequency vibration of an airfoil, usually caused by high speed or poor construction.

Flying stabilizer: A horizontal stabilizer where the entire airfoil, rather than just the elevator, is pivoted for pitch control.

Flying wing: An aircraft design without a stabilizer and a short fuselage or just a cockpit.

Frequency: See *Radio Frequency.*

Fully proportional: A type of radio control where the movement of the controls on the transmitters is duplicated in both angle and speed in the servo motors of the aircraft.

Fuselage: The body of any aircraft.

Gimbal: The control stick on a radio-control transmitter that can be moved in any direction for complete control of two servo motors.

Glider: An engine-less airplane that relies on a launching force or energy to become airborne.

Glide ratio: The number of feet or other units that an aircraft will travel horizontally for each vertical foot or unit of descent.

Glow plug: A device, similar to a spark plug, that is used to ignite the fuel/air mixture in an engine's combustion chamber.

Half-A (½A): A model aircraft engine or class for engines with a displacement of less than .050 cubic inch.

Horizontal stabilizer: The fixed portion of the horizontal flying surface at the rear of an aircraft.

Indoor wood: Balsa wood with exceptionally light weight and strength, used mostly for indoor free-flight model aircraft construction.

Leading edge: The front or forward edge of a wing, stabilizer, rudder, or other flying surface.

Longerons: The structural ribs that run lengthwise in a fuselage. (See also *Stringers.*)

Ni-cads: Rechargeable batteries made primarily of nickel and cadmium.

Nose-block: The portion of a rubber-powered model aircraft that contains the propeller shaft.

Pattern: A type of model aircraft flying competition that includes precise aerobatic maneuvers.

Pitch: The movement of an aircraft up and down about the center of gravity.

Polyhedral: A modification of dihedral where the tip or end portions of the wing angle upward at a greater angle than the center portions of the wing when viewed from the front.

Pot: An electronic devise used in radio control; more correctly, a potentiometer.

Proportional: See *Fully Proportional.*

Pushrod: The wood, metal, or plastic rods that are pivoted on both ends to connect a servo motor wheel or bell crank to the control horn on the flaps or to the throttle lever.

Radio: The electric device that is used to transmit signals from the flier's hand lever controls to the receiver in the aircraft.

Radio frequency: The proper term for the frequencies or signals transmitted by a radio-control transmitter and received by the receiver in the aircraft.

R/C: The symbol used to indicate radio control.

Ribs: The structural members of a wing that connect the leading and trailing edges and provide the airfoil shape.

Roll: The movement (or left and right banking lean) of an aircraft about an axis extending from the nose to the tail and through the center of gravity.

Rudder: The pivoted vertical control surface at the rear of the vertical stabilizer—also used (in error) to describe the entire vertical stabilizer.

Sailplane: An airplane constructed light enough and with enough lift to gain altitude in flight by rising on thermals.

Servo motor: Small electric motors, mounted in the aircraft and controlled by the radio transmitter to move the aircraft's control flaps and throttle.

Sinking speed: The loss of an aircraft's altitude in feet per second in time as measured in still air.

Spar: The main structural members of a wing (other than the leading and trailing edges) that extend inside its span.

Spoiler: The flaps that pivot upward from the top or bottom of a wing to decrease the lift or to increase the drag.

Stabilizer: Usually used to describe the "horizontal stabilizer".

Stress: The unit of force divided by the area that force is acting upon.

Stringers: The smaller longerons in the fuselage.

Thermal: A bubble or current of heated air rising from the surface of the ground or from the roof of a building.

Torque: The tendency of an aircraft to rotate around the axis of the propeller shaft in the opposite direction from the rotation of the propeller.

Trailing edge: The rear edge of a wing, stabilizer, rudder, or other flying surface.

Trim: The micrometer adjustments on a radio-control transmitter that allow adjustment of the control levers' movements of the aircraft control surfaces. Also, the adjustment of any aircraft's flying surfaces for a desired stable flight path.

Trim tabs: Small tabs or control surfaces in or to the rear of the trailing edges of the control surfaces. Used to make small adjustments in the aircraft's flight path.

Undercambered airfoil: An airfoil where both the top and the bottom surfaces curve upward near the center.

Vee tail: A horizontal stabilizer that is angled upward in a "vee" shape when viewed from the front of the aircraft. A vee tail serves the functions of both a vertical stabilizer (rudder) and a horizontal stabilizer.

Vertical stabilizer: The vertical control surface at the rear of the aircraft, sometimes called a "rudder" (in error).

Warp: An intentional twist in the wings or other control surfaces of an aircraft along the span.

Wash-in: A twist or deliberate warp in the wing which results in the forward tip of the wing being higher than the rearward tip.

Wash-out: A twist or deliberate warp in the wing which results in the rearward tip of the wing being higher than the forward tip.

Wind tunnel: A special chamber used to develop an artificial wind for aeronautical experiments.

Wing chord: The width of the wing as measured from the leading to the trailing edge.

Wing loading: The weight of the aircraft divided by the total wing area measured in ounces per square foot.

Yaw: The movement of an aircraft from left to right about a vertical axis through the center of gravity.

Sources of Supply, Publications and Clubs

Sources of Supply

Most of these firms can supply catalogs, and there is often a charge. If you write to any model supply firm requesting the price of their catalog or any other information be sure to enclose a stamped, self-addressed envelope if you expect a reply. You might also mention where you read of the existence of the firm. Many of these firms are part-time businesses operated by hobbyists, and they can use whatever friendly help you can provide. We have listed the general categories of model aircraft supplies that each firm specializes in after its address.

Ace R/C, Inc.
Box 511
Higginsville, MO 64037
Radios, batteries, R/C sport aircraft

Astro Flight, Inc.
13377 Beach Ave.
Venice, CA 90291
Electric motors, hi-starts, sailplanes

Balsa U.S.A.
Box 164
Marinette, WI 54143
Balsa, plywood, hardwood

Byron Originals
P.O. Box 279
Ida Grove, IA 51445
R/C scale aircraft

Cannon Electronics
13400 Saticoy St.
North Hollywood, CA 91605
Radio-control equipment

Cleveland Models & Supply Co.
10307 Detroit Rd.
Cleveland, OH 44102
Outdoor free-flight aircraft

Coverite
420 Babylon Rd.
Horsham, PA 19044
Covering materials

Cox Hobbies
1525 E. Warner Ave.
Santa Ana, CA 92705
Full range of products

Craft-Air
20115 Nordhoff St.
Chatsworth, CA 91311
Sailplanes, R/C trainers

Du-Bro Products
480 Bonner Rd.
Waucoda, IL 60084
Control-line and R/C pushrods

Flyline Models
  P.O. Box 2136
  Fairfax, VA 22031
    Free-flight scale aircraft

Fox Manufacturing Co.
  5305 Towson Ave.
  Fort Smith, AK 72901
    Engines, fuel, accessories

Futaba Industries, U.S.A.
  555 W. Victoria St.
  Compton, CA 90220
    Radio-control equipment

Doug Gailbraith
  707 2nd St.
  Davis, CA 95616
    Free-flight timers and accessories

Carl Goldberg Models
  4738 W. Chicago Ave.
  Chicago, IL 60651
  ◦ *R/C and control-line aircraft and
    accessories*

Gorham Associates
  23961 Craftsman Rd.
  Calabasas, CA 91302
    R/C helicopters

Great Planes Model Mfg. Co.
  P.O. Box 721
  Urbana, IL 61801
    Aircraft kits, radios, parts

Paul K. Guillow, Inc.
  P.O. Box 229
  Wakefield, MA 01880
    *R/C, control-line, and free-flight
    aircraft*

Hi-Flight Model Products
  43225 Whittier Ave.
  Hemet, CA 92343
    Sailplanes, electric winches

Hobby Shack
  18480 Bandalier Cr.
  Fountain Valley, CA 92728-8610
    Imported kits, engines, radios

House of Balsa
  20134 State Rd.
  Cerritos, CA 90701
    R/C sport and scale aircraft

Jemco
  1578 Osage St.
  San Marcos, CA 92069
    R/C scale aircraft

Jetco
  833 Lexington Ave.
  Brooklyn, NY 11221
    Free-flight and R/C sport aircraft

Larry Jolley Concepts
  8380 Kattella Ave.
  Stanton, CA 90680
    R/C helicopters

K & B Manufacturing
  12152 Woodruff Ave.
  Downey, CA 90241
    Engines and fuel

Kavan Model Aircraft, Inc. (see
Hobby Shack)

Kraft Midwest
  117 E. Main St.
  Northville, MI 48167
    Radio-control equipment

Legion Air
  3017 Norwood
  Arlington, TX 76013
  Sailplanes

Litco Systems
  Box 90
  East Hanover, NJ 07936
    Radio-control equipment

Mark's Models
  1578 Osage St.
  San Marcos, CA 92069
    Sailplanes and R/C sport aircraft

Micro-X Models
  Box 1063
  Lorain, OH 44055
    Free-flight aircraft

Midwest Products Corp.
400 S. Indiana St.
Hobart, IN 46342
   R/C and control-line aircraft, ducted fan engines

Miniature Aircraft USA
2324 No. Orange Blossom Trail
Orlando, FL 32804
   R/C helicopters

Model Engineering of Norwalk (M.E.N.)
54 Chestnut Hill
Norwalk, CT 06851
   R/C trainer and sport aircraft

Model Rectifier Corp.
2500 Woodbridge Ave.
Edison, NJ 08817
   Radio-control equipment, engines, R/C aircraft

Bud Nosen Models
Box 105
Two Harbors, MN 55616
   R/C scale aircraft

OS Engines (see Great Planes)

Peck-Polymers
Box 2498
La Mesa, CA 92041
   Free-flight aircraft

Pica
2657 N.E. 188th St.
Miami, FL 33180
   Decals, R/C scale aircraft

Pierce Aero Co.
9626 Jellico Ave.
Northridge, CA 91325
   Sailplanes

Polks Hobbies
346 Bergen Ave.
Jersey City, NJ 07403
   Full range of products

Prather Products
1660 Ravenia Ave.
Wilmington, CA 90744
   R/C pylon aircraft, control-line accessories

RJL Industries
1831 Business Center Dr.
Duarte, CA 91010
   Carburetors, engine accessories

Robbe Modellsport
180 Township Line Rd.
Belle Mead, NJ 08502
   Kits, ARF planes, engines, radios

Rotary Wing Concepts
1010 No. 4th St.
Miamisburg, OH 45342
   R/C helicopters

Royal Electronics
3535 S. Irving
Denver, CO 80110
   Radio-control equipment

Royal Products
2380 So. Holley Pl.
Denver, CO 80222
   R/C scale aircraft, engines

Schluter (see Robbe Modellsport)

Scientific Models
340 Snyder Ave.
Berkeley Heights, NJ 07922
   Control-line and free-flight aircraft

Sig Manufacturing Co.
401 S. Front St.
Montezuma, IA 50171
   Full range of products

Sterling Models
3620 G St.
Philadelphia, PA 19134
   R/C and free-flight aircraft

Testor Corp.
  620 Buckbee St.
  Rockford, IL 61101
    Engines, control-line aircraft

Top Flite Models
  1901 N. Narragansett Ave.
  Chicago, IL 60639
    *R/C and control-line models,
    plastic coverings*

Webra Engines (see Model Rectifier Corp.)

World Engines, Inc.
  8960 Rossash Ave.
  Cincinnati, OH 45236
    Engines

Publications

Magazines

Flying Models
  Box 700
  Newton, NJ 07860
    sample copy $2.25

Model Airplane News
  632 Danbury Rd., Rte. 7
  Georgetown, CT 06829
    sample copy $2.95

Model Aviation
  815 15th St. N.W.
  Washington, DC 20005
    sample copy $1.75

Model Builder
  898 W. 16th St.
  Newport Beach, CA 92663
    sample copy $2.50

Radio Control Modeler
  Box 487
  Sierra Madre, CA 91024
    sample copy $2.25

Plans

  All of the monthly magazines offer scale-model plans for sale, and most issues include at least one scale-model plan. Contact the magazines for catalogs of available plans. These firms also offer scale-model plans for sale:

Model Airplane News Publishing
  632 Danbury Rd.
  Wilton, CT 06897

Modernistic Models
  Box 6974
  Albuquerque, NM 87197

Sid Morgan Vintage Aircraft Plans
  13157 Ormond
  Belleville, MI 48111

SPPS
  3209 Madison Ave.
  Greensboro, NC 27403-1424

Nick Ziroli
  29 Edgar Dr.
  Smithtown, NY 11787

Clubs

Academy of Model Aeronautics
1810 Samuel Morse Dr.
Reston, VA 22091

CL (Control Line) Racing Pilots and Mechanics Association
1122 Plaza Circle
Joppa, MD 21805

FAI Control Line Society
523 Meadowbrook Circle
St. Davids, PA 19087

International Miniature Aerobatics Club
16970 Barnell Ave.
Morgan Hill, CA 95037

League of Silent Flight (R/C sailplanes)
P.O. Box 39068
Chicago, IL 60639

Miniature Aircraft Combat Association
1443 McKinley Ave.
Escondido, CA 92027

Model Engine Collectors Association
P.O. Box 725
Indianapolis, IN 46206

National Association of Rocketry
182 Madison Dr.
Elizabeth, PA 15037

National Free Flight Society
707 Second St.
Davis, CA 95616

National Indoor Model Airplane Society
Box 545
Richardson, TX 75080

National Miniature Pylon Racing Association
4000 Havenhurst Ave.
Encino, CA 91436

National Radio Control Helicopter Association
P.O. Box 487
Sierra Madre, CA 91024

National Soaring Society (R/C sailplanes)
Box 1530
Denver, CO 80220

National Society of Radio Controlled Aerobatics
8534 Huddleston Dr.
Cincinnati, OH 45236

Precision Aerobatic Model Pilots Association (control-line stunt)
1640 Maywick Dr.
Lexington, KY 40504

Society of Antique Modelers
1947 Superior Ave.
Whiting, IN 46394

Index

Page numbers in **bold** type indicate information in illustrations.

"ABC Scrambler," **97**
Academy of Model Aeronautics (AMA), 1–2, 144–145
  rules of, 146, 148, 150
  safety code of, 13
Aerodrome, model, 50, 52, **52**
Aerodynamics, 14–27
  basic principles of, 14–15
  climbing high, 17–18
  complete control, 23–27
  in-flight stability, 19–21
  lighter-than-air paints and skins, 27
  searching for center of gravity, 22–23
Aileron rolls, 87
Ailerons, 20, 23, 25, **25**
Airfoil shape, 15, 17–20
  flat-bottom, 17
  of stabilizer, 19–20
  symmetrical, 17
  undercambered, 15
  of wing, 15, 17–18, **17, 18**
"Alouette 2," 107, **108**
Altitude. *See also* Lift
  plane refusing to gain, 26
"Ambush," 53, **54**
Angle of attack, 18, **18**
  in complete control, 24
"Astro Start," 44
Autorotation feature, **104,** 107, 108–109
Axes. *See* Pitch; Roll; Yaw

"Baby Ace," **95**
"Baby Bee," **29**
Banking, 20, 25
Base leg, 83, **84, 85**
Batteries, connecting to glow plug, **32,** 33
  in electric motors, 39, 42, **42**
  for radio-control rigs, 68
Bearers, 71
Bell crank, 3
"Bell Jet Ranger," **105**
"Bell 222," **109**
Birds, secret of, 15, 17
"Brick," **72**
Buddy box radio transmitter setups, 77
Building. *See* Kit building; Super scale
"Buster," **54**

Carburetor, for internal combustion engine, 28, 29, **35**
Cement, for kit building, 111–112, **116, 117**
  for repairs, 131, **132**
Center of gravity, altering, 21
  determining, 21
  effect of, on stability, 20–21, **20**
  searching for, 22–23
Cessna 182, **138**
Channels, 63–65, **68**
Circuit board receiver, **64**
Cleaning, 133
Clevis links, **73**
Clevises, **121**
Clubs, 143–146
Collective pitch, 110
Collective pitch rotors, 105, **105, 106,** 110
Combat, 61, **61**
"Commander," 107
Competition, 144–146, **145–147,** 152
  examples of stunts performed in, **150–151**
  rules of, 148, 150
Compression stroke, 29, **30**
Contests, 144. *See also* Competition
Control, radio. *See* Radio control
Control flaps, 120, **121**
Control handle, 3
Control horns, 120, **121**
Control-line models, 3–4, **3,** 47–61
  in combat, 61, **61**
  in competition, **149, 150–151**
  control lines of, 52–53
  costs of, 7
  first solo with, 49–50, **51**
  flight line school for use of, 47–49
  model aerodrome for, 50, 52, **52**
  stepping up, 53–56, **54–56**
  stunts for, 56–60, **57–61**
Control-line scale, 139
Control lines, 52–53
  center of gravity affected by, 21, 23
  nylon, 53
  steel, 53
Control surfaces, 23–27
Costs of model aircraft, 5–9
Coverings. *See* Paint; Plastic color coverings

Crashes, avoiding, in radio-control flight, 76–78
    in combat, 61
    repairing damage after, 131, **131, 132,** 133, **133**
"Cub," 64, **64, 79**

Decals, 123, 125, 129, **130,** 131
Dethermalizer, 26, **98, 99,** 100–101
Dihedral, 20
Dive brakes, 27
Diving, cause and remedy for, 26
Downwind (downward) leg, 83, **84, 85**
Drag, angle of attack and, 18
    wing shape and, 15, 17, 18

Electric launching winch, 44–45, **44, 46**
Electric power plants, 39, 42–43, **42**
    selection chart, **41**
"Electric Sportavia," **42**
Elevator, 24, **24**
Energy. *See also* Engine; Power plants
    necessary for flight, 14–15
Engines, 4
    converting to electric power, 42
    diesel, 31
    internal combustion, 28–29, **29, 30,** 31
    problems with, trouble-shooting chart for, 36
    for radio-control aircraft, large, **38**
    selection chart, 38–39, **40–41**
    tow-line, 43–46, **43–46**
    two-stroke, **29, 30,** 31
Epoxies, for kit building, 112, 115, **117**
    for repairs, 131, **131**
Exhaust, **30**
"E-Z Bee," 6, 8, **75, 79**

Fairchild 22, **2**
Federal Aeronautics Administration, on operat-
    ing standards for model aircraft, 12
Fiberglass cloth, 115
Field, for control-line flying, 50, 52, **52**
    for outdoor free flight, 97
    for radio-control flight, 80
Figure eights, in competitions, **151**
    for control-line models, 58–60, **60**
Fillets, 115, **117**
Finishes, 122–133
Fixed-wing flight, 102–103
Flaps, control, 120, **121**
    landing, 27
Flight. *See also* Model aircraft
    basic principles of, 14–15. *See also*
        Aerodynamics
    free. *See* Free flight
    trouble-shooting chart for, 26
Flight line school, 47–49
Flying stabilizer, 24
"Flying Tiger," **55**
Focke-Wulf Fw190, **141**
Free flight models, 2, **6**
    classes for, 90–91
    costs of, 6–7
    indoor, 90, 91, 93–95, **94, 95, 100**
    outdoor, 91, 97, 100–101

peanut and jumbo scale, 91–93
rubber powered, 90, 91, 95, **96,** 97, **100**
trim tabs for, 95, **96**
Frequencies, 65, 68
    chart of, **69**
Frequency pole, 65, 68
Fuel, in engine starting, 31, **32,** 33
    selecting proper, 37
Fuel pickup line, 37
Fuel-proof paint, 128
Fuel tanks, 37
Fuel transfer, **30**

Glider, free-flight, **98,** 100
Glow plugs, 29, **29,** 31, **32,** 33
    effect of racing fuel on, 37
Glue. *See also* Cement; Epoxies
    for tissue paper covering, 122, **123**
Glue joints, instant, 112–113, 115

Half A, 7
Hand, 3
"Hawk," **82**
Heinkel 100D, **93**
"Heli-Baby," 107
"Heli-Boy," **103,** 107, **109**
Helicopters, 102–110
    autorotation capability of, 108–109
    flight of, 109–110
        forward, 104–105
        hovering, 102–103
    radio control, 105, **106,** 107
Hi-Start tow lines, 43–45, **43**
Hinges, 120, **121**

Immelmann turn, 87
Indoor free flight, 90, 91, 93–95, **94, 95, 100**
Inside loop, for control-line models, 58–59, **59**
    in radio-control flight, 88
Insurance, 1–2
Internal combustion engine, 28–29, **29, 30,** 31
Irons, to heat and seal plastic coverings, **125,**
    127–128

"Jet Ranger," 107
Jumbo scale, 91–93, 139

"Kadet," 78
Kits
    building, 111–121, **112–114**
        cement secrets, 111–112, **116–117**
        control flaps, 120, **121**
        epoxies, 115
        instant glue joints, 112–113, 115
        tools, 118, **118,** 119, 120
    control-line model, beginner, 52–53
        second, 53, **54–55,** 56, **56,**
    costs of, 6–9
    for free-flight aircraft, 90–91, 92, **92, 96, 97,**
        100–101
    for models using electric motors, 42
    radio, 69
    radio-control training, 78–79, **79**
    for super scale, **138,** 139, 141

"Kiwi," 8
Knives, 118, **118**, **119**

Landing. *See also* Field
 in radio-control flying, 83–84, **84**–86
Landing flaps, 27
"Launch Pail," 44
Launching winch, electric, 44–45, **44**, **46**
Leadout lines, 53
Letters. *See also* Decals
 tissue paper for, 123
"Libelle," **140**
Lift, produced by angle of attack, 18, **18**
 produced by stabilizer, 20
 wing shape and, 15, 17–18, **18**
"Lightning," **140**
Loops, inside, 58–59, **59**, 88, 150
 outside, 58, 60, **60**, 88, **150**, **151**

"Mach None," **63**
Markings. *See* Decals; Letters
"Mini-Bell," 65
"Miss San Bernardino," **112**
Model aircraft, 1–13
 costs of, 5–9
 forms of, 2–4
 large. *See* Super scale
 power plants for, 4–5. *See also* Power plants
 ready-built. 10–11
 standards for operation of, 12
 true-to-life scale, 11
Motors. *See* Power Plants; Engines
Movements, terms to describe, 20, **20**
Mufflers, 38
Mustang, P-51, **55**, **136**
"Mustang Stunter," **148**

National Association of Rocketry (NAR), 146
National Model Airplane Championships,
  145–146
NATS (national contests), 144, 145, 146
Needle valve, **29**, 31, 33, **34**, 35
"Nesmith Cougar," **135**
Numbers. *See also* Decals
 tissue paper for, 123

"One Night 28," **91**
Operating standards for model aircraft, 12. *See
  also* Rules
Outdoor free flight, 91, 97, 100–101
Outside loops, 58, 60, **60**, 88, **150**, **151**

Paint, clear, 122, 123
 fuel-proof, 128
 lighter-than-air, 27
 other finishes and, 122–133
 techniques for applying, 128–129, **128**, **129**
Pattern flying, 61, 88
Peanut scale, 91–93, 139
Pitch, 20, **20**, 21, 23, 24
 collective, 105, **105**, **106**, 110
"Pitts," **85**
Plastic color coverings, 124–128, **125**–**127**
 for repairs, 131, **132**, 133

Power plants, 4–5, 28–46. *See also* Engines
 electric, 39, 42–43
 engines and propellers, choosing, 38–39, **40**–**41**
 fuel for, selecting proper, 37
 fuel tanks, 37
 internal combustion engine, 28–31
 mufflers, 38
 selection chart, **41**
 starting techniques for, 31–36
 tow-line engines, 43–46
Power stroke, 28, 29, **30**
"Prairie Bird," **6**
Problems. *See* Trouble-shooting charts
Propellers, choosing, 38–39
 charts on, **40**–**41**
Pushrods, 3, 63, 71, **73**
 hardware for, 120, **121**
 of helicopter, **106**

"Q-Tee," 78, **96**
"Quarter Midget," **10**

Radio-control helicopters, 105, **106**, 107
Radio-control models, **2**, 3, 62–89
 advanced techniques in, 84, 86–87
 aileron rolls in, 87
 channels, 63–65, **68**, **70**
 control sticks in, **66**–67
 first aircraft using, 78–80
 first flight using, 80, 82
 frequencies, 65, 68
  chart of, **69**
 fully proportioned, 62, **70**
 landing, 83–84, **84**–**85**
 no-crash system of, 76–78
 pattern flying, 88
 powered aircraft as, costs of, 8–9
  trainer for, **9**
 pulse proportional systems of, 63
 quality bargains for, 69–70
 radios for, 62–63
  installation of, 70–71
 sailplanes as. *See also* Sailplanes
  costs of, 7–8
 servo motor mounts for, 71, **72**–**73**, 74–75
 thermal soaring by, 88–89
 trouble-shooting chart for, 74
Radio-control sailplane, costs of, 7–8
 launching of, 43–45, **45**
Radio-control scale, 139, **140**, 141–142
Radio transmitter setups, buddy box, 77
"Ranger," 78
Ready-built aircraft, 10–11
Reed valve, 28–29, **29**, 30
Repair tips, 131, **131**, **132**, 133, **133**
"Rev-olution," 107
Rivets, flush, 27
Rocky Mountain Soaring Association,
  144, 147
"ROG," **92**
ROG (rise-off-ground) takeoff, 94
Roll(s), 20, **20**, 21
 controlling, 25, **25**
 aileron, 87

Rotor(s), collective pitch, 105, **105, 106,** 110
  helicopter, 104, 105, **105**–107
    in autorotation, 108–109
  tail, 104
Rubber power, in free flight, 90, 91, 95, **96,**
    97, **100**
Rudder, 19, 23, **24**
  in complete control, 23
  in radio-control systems, 71, 74, 75
Rules. *See also* Federal Aeronautics Administra-
    tion; Safety code
  of competition, 146, 148, 150

"S-Tee," 78
Safety code, 13
"Sailaire," **16**
Sailplanes, **82,** 88–89, **89**
  costs of, 7–8
  launching of, 43–45, **45**
Sanding, painting and, 128–129
Sandpaper, 118, **119**
Saws, 120
Scale, cheap, 139
  control-line, 139
  determining, 134
  peanut and jumbo, 91–93, 139
  radio-control, 139, 141–142
  super, 134–142
  true-to-life, 11
Scale effect, 137, 139
Scale performance, 134, 136
Servo motors, 62–63
Skins, plastic, 27
"Sky-Copter," **104**
"Smith Miniplane," **56**
Soaring, thermal, 88–89
Society of Antique Modelers (SAM), 145
Spark plug, 31
"Spirit of St. Louis," **135**
"Spitfire," **113**
Spoilers, 25–26
"Sportavia," 78, **81**
"Electric," **42**
Stability, in-flight, 19–21
  directional, 20
  lateral, 20
  longitudinal, 20
Stabilizer, of tail, 19–20, 23, **24**
  horizontal, 19–20, 24
  vertical, 23
Stall angle, 18
Stalling, cause and remedy for, 26
Standards, operating, 12. *See also* Rules
Starter, coil spring, **33**
Starting techniques, 31–36, **32–35**
Stick models, for free flight, 90–93
Stripes, 123. *See also* Decals
Stuka, **3**
Stunts, in competitions, **150–151**

for control-line models, 56–60, **57–61**
  combat, 61, **61**
  figure eight, 58–60, **60**
  inside loop, 58–59, **59**
  outside loop, 58, 60, **60**
  partial wingover, 56–57, **57, 58**
  pattern, 61
  in radio-control flight, 88
Super scale, 134–142. *See also* Scale
"Super Stunter," 53
Swash plate, 105, **106**

Tail, stability controlled by, 19–20
Tail rotor, 104
Teachers, for radio-control flying, 77–78
Tee pins, **114,** 118
Test gliding, for center of gravity, 23
Thermal, lift by, 15, **16,** 18
Thermal soaring, 88–89
"Thunderbolt," **138**
Timers, 7
Tissue paper covering, 122–124, **123, 124**
Tools, 118, **118, 119,** 120
Tow line engines, 43–46, **43–46**
Tow lines, "Hi-Start," 43–45, **43**
"Trainer Hawk," 78
Trim, for free flight, 91, 92
Trim tabs, 95, **96**
Trouble-shooting charts, engine, 36
  flight, 26
  radio-control systems, 74
True-to-life scale, 11. *See also* Scale
Turns, banked or coordinated, 20, 25
Tweezers, 118
"Twister," **149**

U-control flying. *See* Control-line models

"Velie Monocoupe," **137**

Wakefield-class models, **99,** 100
Wankel rotary combustion engine, 31
Wash-in, 93, 128
Wash-out, 128
Weight, affected by finish, 27
  of free-flight models, 92
Wind, in control-line flying, 50
  in radio-control flight, 80, 83, 84, 86
Wing cord, 18
Wingover
  double reversed, **150**
  partial, 56–57, **57, 58**
Wings, of birds, 15, 17
  shape of, 15, 17–18, **17**
    airfoil, 15, 17–18, **17**
    flat plate, 17
Wire, 118

Yaw, 20, **20,** 21

A CATALOG OF SELECTED

DOVER BOOKS

IN ALL FIELDS OF INTEREST

A CATALOG OF SELECTED DOVER
BOOKS IN ALL FIELDS OF INTEREST

CONCERNING THE SPIRITUAL IN ART, Wassily Kandinsky. Pioneering work by father of abstract art. Thoughts on color theory, nature of art. Analysis of earlier masters. 12 illustrations. 80pp. of text. 5⅜ x 8½. 23411-8 Pa. $4.95

ANIMALS: 1,419 Copyright-Free Illustrations of Mammals, Birds, Fish, Insects, etc., Jim Harter (ed.). Clear wood engravings present, in extremely lifelike poses, over 1,000 species of animals. One of the most extensive pictorial sourcebooks of its kind. Captions. Index. 284pp. 9 x 12. 23766-4 Pa. $14.95

CELTIC ART: The Methods of Construction, George Bain. Simple geometric techniques for making Celtic interlacements, spirals, Kells-type initials, animals, humans, etc. Over 500 illustrations. 160pp. 9 x 12. (USO) 22923-8 Pa. $9.95

AN ATLAS OF ANATOMY FOR ARTISTS, Fritz Schider. Most thorough reference work on art anatomy in the world. Hundreds of illustrations, including selections from works by Vesalius, Leonardo, Goya, Ingres, Michelangelo, others. 593 illustrations. 192pp. 7⅛ x 10¼. 20241-0 Pa. $9.95

CELTIC HAND STROKE-BY-STROKE (Irish Half-Uncial from "The Book of Kells"): An Arthur Baker Calligraphy Manual, Arthur Baker. Complete guide to creating each letter of the alphabet in distinctive Celtic manner. Covers hand position, strokes, pens, inks, paper, more. Illustrated. 48pp. 8¼ x 11. 24336-2 Pa. $3.95

EASY ORIGAMI, John Montroll. Charming collection of 32 projects (hat, cup, pelican, piano, swan, many more) specially designed for the novice origami hobbyist. Clearly illustrated easy-to-follow instructions insure that even beginning papercrafters will achieve successful results. 48pp. 8¼ x 11. 27298-2 Pa. $3.50

THE COMPLETE BOOK OF BIRDHOUSE CONSTRUCTION FOR WOODWORKERS, Scott D. Campbell. Detailed instructions, illustrations, tables. Also data on bird habitat and instinct patterns. Bibliography. 3 tables. 63 illustrations in 15 figures. 48pp. 5¼ x 8½. 24407-5 Pa. $2.50

BLOOMINGDALE'S ILLUSTRATED 1886 CATALOG: Fashions, Dry Goods and Housewares, Bloomingdale Brothers. Famed merchants' extremely rare catalog depicting about 1,700 products: clothing, housewares, firearms, dry goods, jewelry, more. Invaluable for dating, identifying vintage items. Also, copyright-free graphics for artists, designers. Co-published with Henry Ford Museum & Greenfield Village. 160pp. 8¼ x 11. 25780-0 Pa. $10.95

HISTORIC COSTUME IN PICTURES, Braun & Schneider. Over 1,450 costumed figures in clearly detailed engravings–from dawn of civilization to end of 19th century. Captions. Many folk costumes. 256pp. 8⅜ x 11¾. 23150-X Pa. $12.95

BRASS INSTRUMENTS: Their History and Development, Anthony Baines. Authoritative, updated survey of the evolution of trumpets, trombones, bugles, cornets, French horns, tubas and other brass wind instruments. Over 140 illustrations and 48 music examples. Corrected and updated by author. New preface. Bibliography. 320pp. 5⅜ x 8½. 27574-4 Pa. $9.95

HOLLYWOOD GLAMOR PORTRAITS, John Kobal (ed.). 145 photos from 1926-49. Harlow, Gable, Bogart, Bacall; 94 stars in all. Full background on photographers, technical aspects. 160pp. 8⅜ x 11¼. 23352-9 Pa. $12.95

MAX AND MORITZ, Wilhelm Busch. Great humor classic in both German and English. Also 10 other works: "Cat and Mouse," "Plisch and Plumm," etc. 216pp. 5⅜ x 8½. 20181-3 Pa. $6.95

THE RAVEN AND OTHER FAVORITE POEMS, Edgar Allan Poe. Over 40 of the author's most memorable poems: "The Bells," "Ulalume," "Israfel," "To Helen," "The Conqueror Worm," "Eldorado," "Annabel Lee," many more. Alphabetic lists of titles and first lines. 64pp. 5$\frac{3}{16}$ x 8¼. 26685-0 Pa. $1.00

PERSONAL MEMOIRS OF U. S. GRANT, Ulysses Simpson Grant. Intelligent, deeply moving firsthand account of Civil War campaigns, considered by many the finest military memoirs ever written. Includes letters, historic photographs, maps and more. 528pp. 6⅛ x 9¼. 28587-1 Pa. $12.95

AMULETS AND SUPERSTITIONS, E. A. Wallis Budge. Comprehensive discourse on origin, powers of amulets in many ancient cultures: Arab, Persian Babylonian, Assyrian, Egyptian, Gnostic, Hebrew, Phoenician, Syriac, etc. Covers cross, swastika, crucifix, seals, rings, stones, etc. 584pp. 5⅜ x 8½. 23573-4 Pa. $15.95

RUSSIAN STORIES/PYCCKNE PACCKA3bl: A Dual-Language Book, edited by Gleb Struve. Twelve tales by such masters as Chekhov, Tolstoy, Dostoevsky, Pushkin, others. Excellent word-for-word English translations on facing pages, plus teaching and study aids, Russian/English vocabulary, biographical/critical introductions, more. 416pp. 5⅜ x 8½. 26244-8 Pa. $9.95

PHILADELPHIA THEN AND NOW: 60 Sites Photographed in the Past and Present, Kenneth Finkel and Susan Oyama. Rare photographs of City Hall, Logan Square, Independence Hall, Betsy Ross House, other landmarks juxtaposed with contemporary views. Captures changing face of historic city. Introduction. Captions. 128pp. 8¼ x 11. 25790-8 Pa. $9.95

AIA ARCHITECTURAL GUIDE TO NASSAU AND SUFFOLK COUNTIES, LONG ISLAND, The American Institute of Architects, Long Island Chapter, and the Society for the Preservation of Long Island Antiquities. Comprehensive, well-researched and generously illustrated volume brings to life over three centuries of Long Island's great architectural heritage. More than 240 photographs with authoritative, extensively detailed captions. 176pp. 8¼ x 11. 26946-9 Pa. $14.95

NORTH AMERICAN INDIAN LIFE: Customs and Traditions of 23 Tribes, Elsie Clews Parsons (ed.). 27 fictionalized essays by noted anthropologists examine religion, customs, government, additional facets of life among the Winnebago, Crow, Zuni, Eskimo, other tribes. 480pp. 6⅛ x 9¼. 27377-6 Pa. $10.95

FRANK LLOYD WRIGHT'S HOLLYHOCK HOUSE, Donald Hoffmann. Lavishly illustrated, carefully documented study of one of Wright's most controversial residential designs. Over 120 photographs, floor plans, elevations, etc. Detailed perceptive text by noted Wright scholar. Index. 128pp. 9¼ x 10¾. 27133-1 Pa. $11.95

THE MALE AND FEMALE FIGURE IN MOTION: 60 Classic Photographic Sequences, Eadweard Muybridge. 60 true-action photographs of men and women walking, running, climbing, bending, turning, etc., reproduced from rare 19th-century masterpiece. vi + 121pp. 9 x 12. 24745-7 Pa. $10.95

1001 QUESTIONS ANSWERED ABOUT THE SEASHORE, N. J. Berrill and Jacquelyn Berrill. Queries answered about dolphins, sea snails, sponges, starfish, fishes, shore birds, many others. Covers appearance, breeding, growth, feeding, much more. 305pp. 5¼ x 8¼. 23366-9 Pa. $9.95

GUIDE TO OWL WATCHING IN NORTH AMERICA, Donald S. Heintzelman. Superb guide offers complete data and descriptions of 19 species: barn owl, screech owl, snowy owl, many more. Expert coverage of owl-watching equipment, conservation, migrations and invasions, etc. Guide to observing sites. 84 illustrations. xiii + 193pp. 5⅜ x 8½. 27344-X Pa. $8.95

MEDICINAL AND OTHER USES OF NORTH AMERICAN PLANTS: A Historical Survey with Special Reference to the Eastern Indian Tribes, Charlotte Erichsen-Brown. Chronological historical citations document 500 years of usage of plants, trees, shrubs native to eastern Canada, northeastern U.S. Also complete identifying information. 343 illustrations. 544pp. 6½ x 9¼. 25951-X Pa. $12.95

STORYBOOK MAZES, Dave Phillips. 23 stories and mazes on two-page spreads: Wizard of Oz, Treasure Island, Robin Hood, etc. Solutions. 64pp. 8¼ x 11. 23628-5 Pa. $2.95

NEGRO FOLK MUSIC, U.S.A., Harold Courlander. Noted folklorist's scholarly yet readable analysis of rich and varied musical tradition. Includes authentic versions of over 40 folk songs. Valuable bibliography and discography. xi + 324pp. 5⅜ x 8½. 27350-4 Pa. $9.95

MOVIE-STAR PORTRAITS OF THE FORTIES, John Kobal (ed.). 163 glamor, studio photos of 106 stars of the 1940s: Rita Hayworth, Ava Gardner, Marlon Brando, Clark Gable, many more. 176pp. 8⅜ x 11¼. 23546-7 Pa. $14.95

BENCHLEY LOST AND FOUND, Robert Benchley. Finest humor from early 30s, about pet peeves, child psychologists, post office and others. Mostly unavailable elsewhere. 73 illustrations by Peter Arno and others. 183pp. 5⅜ x 8½. 22410-4 Pa. $6.95

YEKL and THE IMPORTED BRIDEGROOM AND OTHER STORIES OF YIDDISH NEW YORK, Abraham Cahan. Film Hester Street based on Yekl (1896). Novel, other stories among first about Jewish immigrants on N.Y.'s East Side. 240pp. 5⅜ x 8½. 22427-9 Pa. $6.95

SELECTED POEMS, Walt Whitman. Generous sampling from *Leaves of Grass*. Twenty-four poems include "I Hear America Singing," "Song of the Open Road," "I Sing the Body Electric," "When Lilacs Last in the Dooryard Bloom'd," "O Captain! My Captain!"–all reprinted from an authoritative edition. Lists of titles and first lines. 128pp. 5³⁄₁₆ x 8¼. 26878-0 Pa. $1.00

THE BEST TALES OF HOFFMANN, E. T. A. Hoffmann. 10 of Hoffmann's most important stories: "Nutcracker and the King of Mice," "The Golden Flowerpot," etc. 458pp. 5⅜ x 8½. 21793-0 Pa. $9.95

FROM FETISH TO GOD IN ANCIENT EGYPT, E. A. Wallis Budge. Rich detailed survey of Egyptian conception of "God" and gods, magic, cult of animals, Osiris, more. Also, superb English translations of hymns and legends. 240 illustrations. 545pp. 5⅜ x 8½. 25803-3 Pa. $13.95

FRENCH STORIES/CONTES FRANÇAIS: A Dual-Language Book, Wallace Fowlie. Ten stories by French masters, Voltaire to Camus: "Micromegas" by Voltaire; "The Atheist's Mass" by Balzac; "Minuet" by de Maupassant; "The Guest" by Camus, six more. Excellent English translations on facing pages. Also French-English vocabulary list, exercises, more. 352pp. 5⅜ x 8½. 26443-2 Pa. $9.95

CHICAGO AT THE TURN OF THE CENTURY IN PHOTOGRAPHS: 122 Historic Views from the Collections of the Chicago Historical Society, Larry A. Viskochil. Rare large-format prints offer detailed views of City Hall, State Street, the Loop, Hull House, Union Station, many other landmarks, circa 1904-1913. Introduction. Captions. Maps. 144pp. 9⅜ x 12¼. 24656-6 Pa. $12.95

OLD BROOKLYN IN EARLY PHOTOGRAPHS, 1865-1929, William Lee Younger. Luna Park, Gravesend race track, construction of Grand Army Plaza, moving of Hotel Brighton, etc. 157 previously unpublished photographs. 165pp. 8⅞ x 11¾. 23587-4 Pa. $13.95

THE MYTHS OF THE NORTH AMERICAN INDIANS, Lewis Spence. Rich anthology of the myths and legends of the Algonquins, Iroquois, Pawnees and Sioux, prefaced by an extensive historical and ethnological commentary. 36 illustrations. 480pp. 5⅜ x 8½. 25967-6 Pa. $10.95

AN ENCYCLOPEDIA OF BATTLES: Accounts of Over 1,560 Battles from 1479 B.C. to the Present, David Eggenberger. Essential details of every major battle in recorded history from the first battle of Megiddo in 1479 B.C. to Grenada in 1984. List of Battle Maps. New Appendix covering the years 1967-1984. Index. 99 illustrations. 544pp. 6½ x 9¼. 24913-1 Pa. $16.95

SAILING ALONE AROUND THE WORLD, Captain Joshua Slocum. First man to sail around the world, alone, in small boat. One of great feats of seamanship told in delightful manner. 67 illustrations. 294pp. 5⅜ x 8½. 20326-3 Pa. $6.95

ANARCHISM AND OTHER ESSAYS, Emma Goldman. Powerful, penetrating, prophetic essays on direct action, role of minorities, prison reform, puritan hypocrisy, violence, etc. 271pp. 5⅜ x 8½. 22484-8 Pa. $7.95

MYTHS OF THE HINDUS AND BUDDHISTS, Ananda K. Coomaraswamy and Sister Nivedita. Great stories of the epics; deeds of Krishna, Shiva, taken from puranas, Vedas, folk tales; etc. 32 illustrations. 400pp. 5⅜ x 8½. 21759-0 Pa. $12.95

BEYOND PSYCHOLOGY, Otto Rank. Fear of death, desire of immortality, nature of sexuality, social organization, creativity, according to Rankian system. 291pp. 5⅜ x 8½. 20485-5 Pa. $8.95

A THEOLOGICO-POLITICAL TREATISE, Benedict Spinoza. Also contains unfinished Political Treatise. Great classic on religious liberty, theory of government on common consent. R. Elwes translation. Total of 421pp. 5⅜ x 8½. 20249-6 Pa. $9.95

MY BONDAGE AND MY FREEDOM, Frederick Douglass. Born a slave, Douglass became outspoken force in antislavery movement. The best of Douglass' autobiographies. Graphic description of slave life. 464pp. 5⅜ x 8½. 22457-0 Pa. $8.95

FOLLOWING THE EQUATOR: A Journey Around the World, Mark Twain. Fascinating humorous account of 1897 voyage to Hawaii, Australia, India, New Zealand, etc. Ironic, bemused reports on peoples, customs, climate, flora and fauna, politics, much more. 197 illustrations. 720pp. 5⅜ x 8½. 26113-1 Pa. $15.95

THE PEOPLE CALLED SHAKERS, Edward D. Andrews. Definitive study of Shakers: origins, beliefs, practices, dances, social organization, furniture and crafts, etc. 33 illustrations. 351pp. 5⅜ x 8½. 21081-2 Pa. $8.95

THE MYTHS OF GREECE AND ROME, H. A. Guerber. A classic of mythology, generously illustrated, long prized for its simple, graphic, accurate retelling of the principal myths of Greece and Rome, and for its commentary on their origins and significance. With 64 illustrations by Michelangelo, Raphael, Titian, Rubens, Canova, Bernini and others. 480pp. 5⅜ x 8½. 27584-1 Pa. $9.95

PSYCHOLOGY OF MUSIC, Carl E. Seashore. Classic work discusses music as a medium from psychological viewpoint. Clear treatment of physical acoustics, auditory apparatus, sound perception, development of musical skills, nature of musical feeling, host of other topics. 88 figures. 408pp. 5⅜ x 8½. 21851-1 Pa. $11.95

THE PHILOSOPHY OF HISTORY, Georg W. Hegel. Great classic of Western thought develops concept that history is not chance but rational process, the evolution of freedom. 457pp. 5⅜ x 8½. 20112-0 Pa. $9.95

THE BOOK OF TEA, Kakuzo Okakura. Minor classic of the Orient: entertaining, charming explanation, interpretation of traditional Japanese culture in terms of tea ceremony. 94pp. 5⅜ x 8½. 20070-1 Pa. $3.95

LIFE IN ANCIENT EGYPT, Adolf Erman. Fullest, most thorough, detailed older account with much not in more recent books, domestic life, religion, magic, medicine, commerce, much more. Many illustrations reproduce tomb paintings, carvings, hieroglyphs, etc. 597pp. 5⅜ x 8½. 22632-8 Pa. $12.95

SUNDIALS, Their Theory and Construction, Albert Waugh. Far and away the best, most thorough coverage of ideas, mathematics concerned, types, construction, adjusting anywhere. Simple, nontechnical treatment allows even children to build several of these dials. Over 100 illustrations. 230pp. 5⅜ x 8½. 22947-5 Pa. $8.95

DYNAMICS OF FLUIDS IN POROUS MEDIA, Jacob Bear. For advanced students of ground water hydrology, soil mechanics and physics, drainage and irrigation engineering, and more. 335 illustrations. Exercises, with answers. 784pp. 6⅛ x 9¼. 65675-6 Pa. $19.95

SONGS OF EXPERIENCE: Facsimile Reproduction with 26 Plates in Full Color, William Blake. 26 full-color plates from a rare 1826 edition. Includes "The Tyger," "London," "Holy Thursday," and other poems. Printed text of poems. 48pp. 5¼ x 7. 24636-1 Pa. $4.95

OLD-TIME VIGNETTES IN FULL COLOR, Carol Belanger Grafton (ed.). Over 390 charming, often sentimental illustrations, selected from archives of Victorian graphics—pretty women posing, children playing, food, flowers, kittens and puppies, smiling cherubs, birds and butterflies, much more. All copyright-free. 48pp. 9¼ x 12¼. 27269-9 Pa. $7.95

PERSPECTIVE FOR ARTISTS, Rex Vicat Cole. Depth, perspective of sky and sea, shadows, much more, not usually covered. 391 diagrams, 81 reproductions of drawings and paintings. 279pp. 5⅜ x 8½.   22487-2 Pa. $7.95

DRAWING THE LIVING FIGURE, Joseph Sheppard. Innovative approach to artistic anatomy focuses on specifics of surface anatomy, rather than muscles and bones. Over 170 drawings of live models in front, back and side views, and in widely varying poses. Accompanying diagrams. 177 illustrations. Introduction. Index. 144pp. 8⅜ x11¼.   26723-7 Pa. $8.95

GOTHIC AND OLD ENGLISH ALPHABETS: 100 Complete Fonts, Dan X. Solo. Add power, elegance to posters, signs, other graphics with 100 stunning copyright-free alphabets: Blackstone, Dolbey, Germania, 97 more–including many lower-case, numerals, punctuation marks. 104pp. 8⅛ x 11.   24695-7 Pa. $8.95

HOW TO DO BEADWORK, Mary White. Fundamental book on craft from simple projects to five-bead chains and woven works. 106 illustrations. 142pp. 5⅜ x 8.
          20697-1 Pa. $5.95

THE BOOK OF WOOD CARVING, Charles Marshall Sayers. Finest book for beginners discusses fundamentals and offers 34 designs. "Absolutely first rate . . . well thought out and well executed."–E. J. Tangerman. 118pp. 7¾ x 10⅝.
          23654-4 Pa. $7.95

ILLUSTRATED CATALOG OF CIVIL WAR MILITARY GOODS: Union Army Weapons, Insignia, Uniform Accessories, and Other Equipment, Schuyler, Hartley, and Graham. Rare, profusely illustrated 1846 catalog includes Union Army uniform and dress regulations, arms and ammunition, coats, insignia, flags, swords, rifles, etc. 226 illustrations. 160pp. 9 x 12.   24939-5 Pa. $10.95

WOMEN'S FASHIONS OF THE EARLY 1900s: An Unabridged Republication of "New York Fashions, 1909," National Cloak & Suit Co. Rare catalog of mail-order fashions documents women's and children's clothing styles shortly after the turn of the century. Captions offer full descriptions, prices. Invaluable resource for fashion, costume historians. Approximately 725 illustrations. 128pp. 8⅜ x 11¼.
          27276-1 Pa. $11.95

THE 1912 AND 1915 GUSTAV STICKLEY FURNITURE CATALOGS, Gustav Stickley. With over 200 detailed illustrations and descriptions, these two catalogs are essential reading and reference materials and identification guides for Stickley furniture. Captions cite materials, dimensions and prices. 112pp. 6½ x 9¼.
          26676-1 Pa. $9.95

EARLY AMERICAN LOCOMOTIVES, John H. White, Jr. Finest locomotive engravings from early 19th century: historical (1804–74), main-line (after 1870), special, foreign, etc. 147 plates. 142pp. 11⅜ x 8¼.   22772-3 Pa. $10.95

THE TALL SHIPS OF TODAY IN PHOTOGRAPHS, Frank O. Braynard. Lavishly illustrated tribute to nearly 100 majestic contemporary sailing vessels: Amerigo Vespucci, Clearwater, Constitution, Eagle, Mayflower, Sea Cloud, Victory, many more. Authoritative captions provide statistics, background on each ship. 190 black-and-white photographs and illustrations. Introduction. 128pp. 8⅞ x 11¾.
          27163-3 Pa. $14.95

EARLY NINETEENTH-CENTURY CRAFTS AND TRADES, Peter Stockham (ed.). Extremely rare 1807 volume describes to youngsters the crafts and trades of the day: brickmaker, weaver, dressmaker, bookbinder, ropemaker, saddler, many more. Quaint prose, charming illustrations for each craft. 20 black-and-white line illustrations. 192pp. 4⅝ x 6. 27293-1 Pa. $4.95

VICTORIAN FASHIONS AND COSTUMES FROM HARPER'S BAZAR, 1867–1898, Stella Blum (ed.). Day costumes, evening wear, sports clothes, shoes, hats, other accessories in over 1,000 detailed engravings. 320pp. 9⅜ x 12¼. 22990-4 Pa. $15.95

GUSTAV STICKLEY, THE CRAFTSMAN, Mary Ann Smith. Superb study surveys broad scope of Stickley's achievement, especially in architecture. Design philosophy, rise and fall of the Craftsman empire, descriptions and floor plans for many Craftsman houses, more. 86 black-and-white halftones. 31 line illustrations. Introduction 208pp. 6½ x 9¼. 27210-9 Pa. $9.95

THE LONG ISLAND RAIL ROAD IN EARLY PHOTOGRAPHS, Ron Ziel. Over 220 rare photos, informative text document origin (1844) and development of rail service on Long Island. Vintage views of early trains, locomotives, stations, passengers, crews, much more. Captions. 8⅞ x 11¾. 26301-0 Pa. $13.95

THE BOOK OF OLD SHIPS: From Egyptian Galleys to Clipper Ships, Henry B. Culver. Superb, authoritative history of sailing vessels, with 80 magnificent line illustrations. Galley, bark, caravel, longship, whaler, many more. Detailed, informative text on each vessel by noted naval historian. Introduction. 256pp. 5⅜ x 8½. 27332-6 Pa. $7.95

TEN BOOKS ON ARCHITECTURE, Vitruvius. The most important book ever written on architecture. Early Roman aesthetics, technology, classical orders, site selection, all other aspects. Morgan translation. 331pp. 5⅜ x 8½. 20645-9 Pa. $8.95

THE HUMAN FIGURE IN MOTION, Eadweard Muybridge. More than 4,500 stopped-action photos, in action series, showing undraped men, women, children jumping, lying down, throwing, sitting, wrestling, carrying, etc. 390pp. 7⅞ x 10⅝. 20204-6 Clothbd. $27.95

TREES OF THE EASTERN AND CENTRAL UNITED STATES AND CANADA, William M. Harlow. Best one-volume guide to 140 trees. Full descriptions, woodlore, range, etc. Over 600 illustrations. Handy size. 288pp. 4½ x 6⅜. 20395-6 Pa. $6.95

SONGS OF WESTERN BIRDS, Dr. Donald J. Borror. Complete song and call repertoire of 60 western species, including flycatchers, juncoes, cactus wrens, many more—includes fully illustrated booklet. Cassette and manual 99913-0 $8.95

GROWING AND USING HERBS AND SPICES, Milo Miloradovich. Versatile handbook provides all the information needed for cultivation and use of all the herbs and spices available in North America. 4 illustrations. Index. Glossary. 236pp. 5⅜ x 8½. 25058-X Pa. $7.95

BIG BOOK OF MAZES AND LABYRINTHS, Walter Shepherd. 50 mazes and labyrinths in all—classical, solid, ripple, and more—in one great volume. Perfect inexpensive puzzler for clever youngsters. Full solutions. 112pp. 8⅛ x 11. 22951-3 Pa. $4.95

PIANO TUNING, J. Cree Fischer. Clearest, best book for beginner, amateur. Simple repairs, raising dropped notes, tuning by easy method of flattened fifths. No previous skills needed. 4 illustrations. 201pp. 5⅜ x 8½. 23267-0 Pa. $6.95

A SOURCE BOOK IN THEATRICAL HISTORY, A. M. Nagler. Contemporary observers on acting, directing, make-up, costuming, stage props, machinery, scene design, from Ancient Greece to Chekhov. 611pp. 5⅜ x 8½. 20515-0 Pa. $12.95

THE COMPLETE NONSENSE OF EDWARD LEAR, Edward Lear. All nonsense limericks, zany alphabets, Owl and Pussycat, songs, nonsense botany, etc., illustrated by Lear. Total of 320pp. 5⅜ x 8½. (USO) 20167-8 Pa. $7.95

VICTORIAN PARLOUR POETRY: An Annotated Anthology, Michael R. Turner. 117 gems by Longfellow, Tennyson, Browning, many lesser-known poets. "The Village Blacksmith," "Curfew Must Not Ring Tonight," "Only a Baby Small," dozens more, often difficult to find elsewhere. Index of poets, titles, first lines. xxiii + 325pp. 5⅜ x 8¼. 27044-0 Pa. $8.95

DUBLINERS, James Joyce. Fifteen stories offer vivid, tightly focused observations of the lives of Dublin's poorer classes. At least one, "The Dead," is considered a masterpiece. Reprinted complete and unabridged from standard edition. 160pp. 5³⁄₁₆ x 8¼. 26870-5 Pa. $1.00

THE HAUNTED MONASTERY and THE CHINESE MAZE MURDERS, Robert van Gulik. Two full novels by van Gulik, set in 7th-century China, continue adventures of Judge Dee and his companions. An evil Taoist monastery, seemingly supernatural events; overgrown topiary maze hides strange crimes. 27 illustrations. 328pp. 5⅜ x 8½. 23502-5 Pa. $8.95

THE BOOK OF THE SACRED MAGIC OF ABRAMELIN THE MAGE, translated by S. MacGregor Mathers. Medieval manuscript of ceremonial magic. Basic document in Aleister Crowley, Golden Dawn groups. 268pp. 5⅜ x 8½. 23211-5 Pa. $9.95

NEW RUSSIAN-ENGLISH AND ENGLISH-RUSSIAN DICTIONARY, M. A. O'Brien. This is a remarkably handy Russian dictionary, containing a surprising amount of information, including over 70,000 entries. 366pp. 4½ x 6⅛. 20208-9 Pa. $10.95

HISTORIC HOMES OF THE AMERICAN PRESIDENTS, Second, Revised Edition, Irvin Haas. A traveler's guide to American Presidential homes, most open to the public, depicting and describing homes occupied by every American President from George Washington to George Bush. With visiting hours, admission charges, travel routes. 175 photographs. Index. 160pp. 8¼ x 11. 26751-2 Pa. $11.95

NEW YORK IN THE FORTIES, Andreas Feininger. 162 brilliant photographs by the well-known photographer, formerly with *Life* magazine. Commuters, shoppers, Times Square at night, much else from city at its peak. Captions by John von Hartz. 181pp. 9¼ x 10¾. 23585-8 Pa. $13.95

INDIAN SIGN LANGUAGE, William Tomkins. Over 525 signs developed by Sioux and other tribes. Written instructions and diagrams. Also 290 pictographs. 111pp. 6⅛ x 9¼. 22029-X Pa. $3.95

ANATOMY: A Complete Guide for Artists, Joseph Sheppard. A master of figure drawing shows artists how to render human anatomy convincingly. Over 460 illustrations. 224pp. 8⅜ x 11¼. 27279-6 Pa. $11.95

MEDIEVAL CALLIGRAPHY: Its History and Technique, Marc Drogin. Spirited history, comprehensive instruction manual covers 13 styles (ca. 4th century thru 15th). Excellent photographs; directions for duplicating medieval techniques with modern tools. 224pp. 8⅜ x 11¼. 26142-5 Pa. $12.95

DRIED FLOWERS: How to Prepare Them, Sarah Whitlock and Martha Rankin. Complete instructions on how to use silica gel, meal and borax, perlite aggregate, sand and borax, glycerine and water to create attractive permanent flower arrangements. 12 illustrations. 32pp. 5⅜ x 8½. 21802-3 Pa. $1.00

EASY-TO-MAKE BIRD FEEDERS FOR WOODWORKERS, Scott D. Campbell. Detailed, simple-to-use guide for designing, constructing, caring for and using feeders. Text, illustrations for 12 classic and contemporary designs. 96pp. 5⅜ x 8½. 25847-5 Pa. $3.95

SCOTTISH WONDER TALES FROM MYTH AND LEGEND, Donald A. Mackenzie. 16 lively tales tell of giants rumbling down mountainsides, of a magic wand that turns stone pillars into warriors, of gods and goddesses, evil hags, powerful forces and more. 240pp. 5⅜ x 8½. 29677-6 Pa. $6.95

THE HISTORY OF UNDERCLOTHES, C. Willett Cunnington and Phyllis Cunnington. Fascinating, well-documented survey covering six centuries of English undergarments, enhanced with over 100 illustrations: 12th-century laced-up bodice, footed long drawers (1795), 19th-century bustles, l9th-century corsets for men, Victorian "bust improvers," much more. 272pp. 5⅜ x 8¼. 27124-2 Pa. $9.95

ARTS AND CRAFTS FURNITURE: The Complete Brooks Catalog of 1912, Brooks Manufacturing Co. Photos and detailed descriptions of more than 150 now very collectible furniture designs from the Arts and Crafts movement depict davenports, settees, buffets, desks, tables, chairs, bedsteads, dressers and more, all built of solid, quarter-sawed oak. Invaluable for students and enthusiasts of antiques, Americana and the decorative arts. 80pp. 6½ x 9¼. 27471-3 Pa. $8.95

HOW WE INVENTED THE AIRPLANE: An Illustrated History, Orville Wright. Fascinating firsthand account covers early experiments, construction of planes and motors, first flights, much more. Introduction and commentary by Fred C. Kelly. 76 photographs. 96pp. 8¼ x 11. 25662-6 Pa. $8.95

THE ARTS OF THE SAILOR: Knotting, Splicing and Ropework, Hervey Garrett Smith. Indispensable shipboard reference covers tools, basic knots and useful hitches; handsewing and canvas work, more. Over 100 illustrations. Delightful reading for sea lovers. 256pp. 5⅜ x 8½. 26440-8 Pa. $8.95

FRANK LLOYD WRIGHT'S FALLINGWATER: The House and Its History, Second, Revised Edition, Donald Hoffmann. A total revision–both in text and illustrations–of the standard document on Fallingwater, the boldest, most personal architectural statement of Wright's mature years, updated with valuable new material from the recently opened Frank Lloyd Wright Archives. "Fascinating"–*The New York Times*. 116 illustrations. 128pp. 9¼ x 10¾. 27430-6 Pa. $12.95

PHOTOGRAPHIC SKETCHBOOK OF THE CIVIL WAR, Alexander Gardner. 100 photos taken on field during the Civil War. Famous shots of Manassas Harper's Ferry, Lincoln, Richmond, slave pens, etc. 244pp. 10⅝ x 8¼.   22731-6 Pa. $10.95

FIVE ACRES AND INDEPENDENCE, Maurice G. Kains. Great back-to-the-land classic explains basics of self-sufficient farming. The one book to get. 95 illustrations. 397pp. 5⅜ x 8½.   20974-1 Pa. $7.95

SONGS OF EASTERN BIRDS, Dr. Donald J. Borror. Songs and calls of 60 species most common to eastern U.S.: warblers, woodpeckers, flycatchers, thrushes, larks, many more in high-quality recording.   Cassette and manual 99912-2 $9.95

A MODERN HERBAL, Margaret Grieve. Much the fullest, most exact, most useful compilation of herbal material. Gigantic alphabetical encyclopedia, from aconite to zedoary, gives botanical information, medical properties, folklore, economic uses, much else. Indispensable to serious reader. 161 illustrations. 888pp. 6½ x 9¼. 2-vol. set. (USO)   Vol. I: 22798-7 Pa. $9.95
Vol. II: 22799-5 Pa. $9.95

HIDDEN TREASURE MAZE BOOK, Dave Phillips. Solve 34 challenging mazes accompanied by heroic tales of adventure. Evil dragons, people-eating plants, blood-thirsty giants, many more dangerous adversaries lurk at every twist and turn. 34 mazes, stories, solutions. 48pp. 8¼ x 11.   24566-7 Pa. $2.95

LETTERS OF W. A. MOZART, Wolfgang A. Mozart. Remarkable letters show bawdy wit, humor, imagination, musical insights, contemporary musical world; includes some letters from Leopold Mozart. 276pp. 5⅜ x 8½.   22859-2 Pa. $7.95

BASIC PRINCIPLES OF CLASSICAL BALLET, Agrippina Vaganova. Great Russian theoretician, teacher explains methods for teaching classical ballet. 118 illustrations. 175pp. 5⅜ x 8½.   22036-2 Pa. $5.95

THE JUMPING FROG, Mark Twain. Revenge edition. The original story of The Celebrated Jumping Frog of Calaveras County, a hapless French translation, and Twain's hilarious "retranslation" from the French. 12 illustrations. 66pp. 5⅜ x 8½.
22686-7 Pa. $3.95

BEST REMEMBERED POEMS, Martin Gardner (ed.). The 126 poems in this superb collection of 19th- and 20th-century British and American verse range from Shelley's "To a Skylark" to the impassioned "Renascence" of Edna St. Vincent Millay and to Edward Lear's whimsical "The Owl and the Pussycat." 224pp. 5⅜ x 8½.
27165-X Pa. $5.95

COMPLETE SONNETS, William Shakespeare. Over 150 exquisite poems deal with love, friendship, the tyranny of time, beauty's evanescence, death and other themes in language of remarkable power, precision and beauty. Glossary of archaic terms. 80pp. 5³⁄₁₆ x 8¼.   26686-9 Pa. $1.00

BODIES IN A BOOKSHOP, R. T. Campbell. Challenging mystery of blackmail and murder with ingenious plot and superbly drawn characters. In the best tradition of British suspense fiction. 192pp. 5⅜ x 8½.   24720-1 Pa. $6.95

THE WIT AND HUMOR OF OSCAR WILDE, Alvin Redman (ed.). More than 1,000 ripostes, paradoxes, wisecracks: Work is the curse of the drinking classes; I can resist everything except temptation; etc. 258pp. 5⅜ x 8½. 20602-5 Pa. $6.95

SHAKESPEARE LEXICON AND QUOTATION DICTIONARY, Alexander Schmidt. Full definitions, locations, shades of meaning in every word in plays and poems. More than 50,000 exact quotations. 1,485pp. 6½ x 9¼. 2-vol. set.
Vol. 1: 22726-X Pa. $17.95
Vol. 2: 22727-8 Pa. $17.95

SELECTED POEMS, Emily Dickinson. Over 100 best-known, best-loved poems by one of America's foremost poets, reprinted from authoritative early editions. No comparable edition at this price. Index of first lines. 64pp. 5³⁄₁₆ x 8¼.
26466-1 Pa. $1.00

CELEBRATED CASES OF JUDGE DEE (DEE GOONG AN), translated by Robert van Gulik. Authentic 18th-century Chinese detective novel; Dee and associates solve three interlocked cases. Led to van Gulik's own stories with same characters. Extensive introduction. 9 illustrations. 237pp. 5⅜ x 8½. 23337-5 Pa. $7.95

THE MALLEUS MALEFICARUM OF KRAMER AND SPRENGER, translated by Montague Summers. Full text of most important witchhunter's "bible," used by both Catholics and Protestants. 278pp. 6⅝ x 10. 22802-9 Pa. $12.95

SPANISH STORIES/CUENTOS ESPAÑOLES: A Dual-Language Book, Angel Flores (ed.). Unique format offers 13 great stories in Spanish by Cervantes, Borges, others. Faithful English translations on facing pages. 352pp. 5⅜ x 8½.
25399-6 Pa. $8.95

THE CHICAGO WORLD'S FAIR OF 1893: A Photographic Record, Stanley Appelbaum (ed.). 128 rare photos show 200 buildings, Beaux-Arts architecture, Midway, original Ferris Wheel, Edison's kinetoscope, more. Architectural emphasis; full text. 116pp. 8¼ x 11. 23990-X Pa. $9.95

OLD QUEENS, N.Y., IN EARLY PHOTOGRAPHS, Vincent F. Seyfried and William Asadorian. Over 160 rare photographs of Maspeth, Jamaica, Jackson Heights, and other areas. Vintage views of DeWitt Clinton mansion, 1939 World's Fair and more. Captions. 192pp. 8⅞ x 11. 26358-4 Pa. $12.95

CAPTURED BY THE INDIANS: 15 Firsthand Accounts, 1750-1870, Frederick Drimmer. Astounding true historical accounts of grisly torture, bloody conflicts, relentless pursuits, miraculous escapes and more, by people who lived to tell the tale. 384pp. 5⅜ x 8½. 24901-8 Pa. $8.95

THE WORLD'S GREAT SPEECHES, Lewis Copeland and Lawrence W. Lamm (eds.). Vast collection of 278 speeches of Greeks to 1970. Powerful and effective models; unique look at history. 842pp. 5⅜ x 8½. 20468-5 Pa. $14.95

THE BOOK OF THE SWORD, Sir Richard F. Burton. Great Victorian scholar/adventurer's eloquent, erudite history of the "queen of weapons"—from prehistory to early Roman Empire. Evolution and development of early swords, variations (sabre, broadsword, cutlass, scimitar, etc.), much more. 336pp. 6⅛ x 9¼.
25434-8 Pa. $9.95

CATALOG OF DOVER BOOKS

THE INFLUENCE OF SEA POWER UPON HISTORY, 1660–1783, A. T. Mahan. Influential classic of naval history and tactics still used as text in war colleges. First paperback edition. 4 maps. 24 battle plans. 640pp. 5⅜ x 8½. 25509-3 Pa. $14.95

THE STORY OF THE TITANIC AS TOLD BY ITS SURVIVORS, Jack Winocour (ed.). What it was really like. Panic, despair, shocking inefficiency, and a little heroism. More thrilling than any fictional account. 26 illustrations. 320pp. 5⅜ x 8½. 20610-6 Pa. $8.95

FAIRY AND FOLK TALES OF THE IRISH PEASANTRY, William Butler Yeats (ed.). Treasury of 64 tales from the twilight world of Celtic myth and legend: "The Soul Cages," "The Kildare Pooka," "King O'Toole and his Goose," many more. Introduction and Notes by W. B. Yeats. 352pp. 5⅜ x 8½. 26941-8 Pa. $8.95

BUDDHIST MAHAYANA TEXTS, E. B. Cowell and Others (eds.). Superb, accurate translations of basic documents in Mahayana Buddhism, highly important in history of religions. The Buddha-karita of Asvaghosha, Larger Sukhavativyuha, more. 448pp. 5⅜ x 8½. 25552-2 Pa. $12.95

ONE TWO THREE . . . INFINITY: Facts and Speculations of Science, George Gamow. Great physicist's fascinating, readable overview of contemporary science: number theory, relativity, fourth dimension, entropy, genes, atomic structure, much more. 128 illustrations. Index. 352pp. 5⅜ x 8½. 25664-2 Pa. $8.95

ENGINEERING IN HISTORY, Richard Shelton Kirby, et al. Broad, nontechnical survey of history's major technological advances: birth of Greek science, industrial revolution, electricity and applied science, 20th-century automation, much more. 181 illustrations. ". . . excellent . . ."–*Isis*. Bibliography. vii + 530pp. 5⅝ x 8¼. 26412-2 Pa. $14.95

DALÍ ON MODERN ART: The Cuckolds of Antiquated Modern Art, Salvador Dalí. Influential painter skewers modern art and its practitioners. Outrageous evaluations of Picasso, Cézanne, Turner, more. 15 renderings of paintings discussed. 44 calligraphic decorations by Dalí. 96pp. 5⅜ x 8½. (USO) 29220-7 Pa. $4.95

ANTIQUE PLAYING CARDS: A Pictorial History, Henry René D'Allemagne. Over 900 elaborate, decorative images from rare playing cards (14th–20th centuries): Bacchus, death, dancing dogs, hunting scenes, royal coats of arms, players cheating, much more. 96pp. 9¼ x 12¼. 29265-7 Pa. $12.95

MAKING FURNITURE MASTERPIECES: 30 Projects with Measured Drawings, Franklin H. Gottshall. Step-by-step instructions, illustrations for constructing handsome, useful pieces, among them a Sheraton desk, Chippendale chair, Spanish desk, Queen Anne table and a William and Mary dressing mirror. 224pp. 8⅛ x 11¼. 29338-6 Pa. $13.95

THE FOSSIL BOOK: A Record of Prehistoric Life, Patricia V. Rich et al. Profusely illustrated definitive guide covers everything from single-celled organisms and dinosaurs to birds and mammals and the interplay between climate and man. Over 1,500 illustrations. 760pp. 7½ x 10⅛. 29371-8 Pa. $29.95

Prices subject to change without notice.

Available at your book dealer or write for free catalog to Dept. GI, Dover Publications, Inc., 31 East 2nd St., Mineola, N.Y. 11501. Dover publishes more than 500 books each year on science, elementary and advanced mathematics, biology, music, art, literary history, social sciences and other areas.